Multiple Intelligences Centers and Projects

Carolyn Chapman

Lynn Freeman

IRI/Skylight Training and Publishing, Inc.
Arlington Heights, Illinois

Multiple Intelligences Centers and Projects

Published by IRI/Skylight Training and Publishing, Inc.
2626 S. Clearbrook Dr.
Arlington Heights, Illinois 60005
Phone 800-348-4474, 847-290-6600
Fax 847-290-6609
irisky@xnet.com
http://www.business1.com/iri_sky/

Creative Director: Robin Fogarty
Managing Editor: Julia E. Noblitt
Editors: Monica Phillips, Patricia Cone
Proofreader: Katherine Schneider
Writers: Amy Wolgemuth, Sabine Vorkoeper
Type Compositor: Donna Ramirez
Book Designers: Bruce Leckie, Susan Price
Formatters: Susan Price, Heidi Ray
Production Supervisor: Bob Crump

ISBN 1-57517-015-9
LCCCN 96-75264

1505-6-96V
Item Number 1449

Dedication

To all the teachers who inspire students
by using knowledge in a way that
personalizes the learning experience.

And, to all the students we have taught.
Our children are our greatest resource,
and they deserve the best we can offer in
quality instruction.

Contents

Introduction

Since the 1983 publication of Howard Gardner's *Frames of Mind: The Theory of Multiple Intelligences,* it has come to the attention of teachers, parents, and students that individuals have more than one intelligence. Although in the history of education and educational testing only two of the intelligences—the verbal/linguistic and the logical/mathematical—have been emphasized, more and more schools are attempting to provide students with the opportunity to explore and develop all of their intelligences. Gardner has identified the following: verbal/linguistic, musical/rhythmic, logical/mathematical, visual/spatial, bodily/kinesthetic, interpersonal, and intrapersonal. (See the Afterword for a short discussion of a possible eighth intelligence.)

Once the theory of multiple intelligences is embraced by a teacher or school, it can be applied in the mind-centered classroom, which permits students to develop and strengthen all of their intelligences by emphasizing the process as much as the product of learning. Classroom centers and projects make the development of students' intelligences possible by providing opportunities to engage in activities that target specific intelligences.

Centers provide the opportunity for students to explore, discover, think, and make decisions in either an open-ended, exploratory setting, in which the teacher is a manager and elicits self-reflection, or in a structured setting, in which the teacher sets specific goals and explains the procedure for the activity.

Projects, on the other hand, provide students with the opportunity to explore a content-related subject in depth, with teacher approval and specific criteria and expectations defined at the outset.

This book is designed to guide you successfully through the process of using centers and projects by providing choices for the students. It is divided into two sections—Section One: Getting Started provides the background and the how-to of multiple intelligences centers and projects and Section Two: Putting It All Together consists of sample projects and centers that deal with six units of study.

Chapter 1 reviews the multiple intelligences—the framework in which the centers and the projects are presented in this book. The next two chapters focus on centers. Chapter 2, "About Centers," guides you through the process of establishing centers, and includes ways to assess whether or not a center is successful, tips for maintaining discipline in centers, and methods for assessing a student's center time using conferencing and student self-assessment. Chapter 3, "Exploratory Centers," provides ideas for exploratory centers that will familiarize you and your students with the process of centers. Each center can be tailored to suit the abilities and needs of your students, as well as your material resources. The center ideas are listed according to targeted intelligence and include a materials list when appropriate.

Chapters 4 and 5 address the how-to of projects. Chapter 4 takes you step-by-step through establishing and managing projects, covering everything from choosing the type of project to celebrating the results. Chapter 5, "Picture-Essay Project," is a detailed account of an ideal first project that will ease you and your students into the *process* of projects.

Section Two: Putting It All Together consists of six chapters, each of which includes center activities and projects for a different unit of focus—the brain, ocean life, pirates and discovery, space, colors, and critters. Each chapter includes a selection of exploratory and structured centers and projects, some of which focus on the specific content area, such as the shark-related projects in Chapter 7, "Discoveries of the Deep Oceans."

These sample centers and projects are designed to enhance the unit of study covered in class and can be customized to suit a variety of student ages. Although each project and center is listed under a targeted intelligence, supporting intelligences are also called into play. By labeling the activities instead of the students, the teacher can set up appropriate learning opportunities that reflect students' interests and needs.

Two appendixes are included, and an afterword that briefly describes an eighth intelligence—the naturalist intelligence.

As you dig into the centers and projects, feel free to adapt the material to the personal interests and skills of both your students and you. Explore ways for students to demonstrate their ideas and abilities using multiple intelligences through these integrated themes. *Multiple Intelligences Centers and Projects* offers a fresh approach to personalizing the learning experience for you and your students, and more than one way of learning in the mind-centered classroom.

IRI/Skylight Training and Publishing, Inc.

SECTION ONE

Getting Started

The Multiple Intelligences

One of the many misconceptions about intelligence is that it is fixed—that individuals live and die with the same intelligence they were born with. According to Alfred Binet, intelligence is the ability to use language and do mathematics. Whole educational systems were built on Binet's understanding. His tests marked the student for life. From this single score, a permanent tattoo was imprinted on each student (Gardner 1993, Chapter 1).

As the inner frontier of the human brain continues to be explored, educators are drawn to its mystery. Reuven Feuerstein and his associates (1980) pioneered the work of cognitive modifiability through cognitive mediation. Roger Sperry investigated the different ways the right and left sides of the brain process. Paul McLean provided insight into the triune brain. Robert Sternberg (1985), Stephen Ceci (1990), and David Feldman (1986) studied the different types of intelligences and asserted that intelligence can be taught. The development of each intelligence depends on how the individual is nurtured.

■ Gardner's Theory of Multiple Intelligences

Howard Gardner's theory of multiple intelligences holds that every individual possesses several different and independent capacities for solving problems and creating products. Intelligence, according to this theory, is defined as the ability to solve problems in a particular cultural setting. Gardner's theory of multiple intelligences includes the following four premises (Gardner 1983).

1. **There is more than one intelligence.** Gardner has named seven, but he concedes there may be more (see fig. 1.1 and the Afterword).

2. **Intelligence can be taught.** Areas of weakness and strength can be improved. Intelligences proceed in stages of development from novice to expert—for example, from the appreciator of music to the virtuoso violinist. This developmental process includes four stages: (1) the first exposure that activates the senses, (2) the opportunity to explore and strengthen the intelligence, (3) the formal training of the intelligence through the guidance of teachers and parents, and (4) the "embrace" or the mastery of the intelligence.

3. **A brain is as unique as a fingerprint.** Each person is born with all intelligences. These intelligences are developed through life's journey of learning, experiences, opportunities, influences, and schooling. Every person has areas of strength and weakness (see fig. 1.2).

4. **Intelligences are forever changing throughout life.** Ability and desire change weaknesses and strengths. Teachers must recognize this fact and expect their students to learn. They must believe that every child can learn. Not only must teachers have high expectations for their students, the students must also have a willingness to learn. It is true that "you can lead a horse to water, but you can't make him drink." The learner has to be stimulated and motivated to understand how the new information will fit into his or her repertoire.

What Is Intelligence According to Gardner?

Gardner defines intelligence as the ability to solve problems and create products valued in a particular cultural setting. He maintains that every individual possesses several different and independent capacities for solving problems and creating products. Let's look at this idea more closely.

Intelligence Is the Ability to Solve a Problem

When two children play a board game and follow the rules step by step, they are solving a problem. People often use their strongest intelligences to solve problems. For example, a person with a strong logical/mathematical intelligence uses words and numbers to give directions. A person with a strong visual/spatial intelligence might give directions using visual cues, such as landmarks. When we use our strong intelligences, problem solving seems natural and easy.

Gardner's Multiple Intelligences

Language Related	Object Related	Person Related
Verbal/Linguistic	Logical/Mathematical	Intrapersonal
Musical/Rhythmic	Visual/Spatial	Interpersonal
	Bodily/Kinesthetic	

Figure 1.1

One Possible Brain Puzzle

The puzzle pieces represent an example of an individual's intelligence areas. They are not meant to indicate a physical location but relative strengths and weaknesses. For example, this individual is most comfortable using the visual/spatial, interpersonal, and verbal/linguistic intelligences. As a teacher, this individual would tend to believe in and practice cooperative learning, emphasize language arts, use props and visuals, and have students engage in hands-on projects. These are all important strategies in a learner-centered classroom, but teachers must be able to involve students whose preferred intelligences differ from their own.

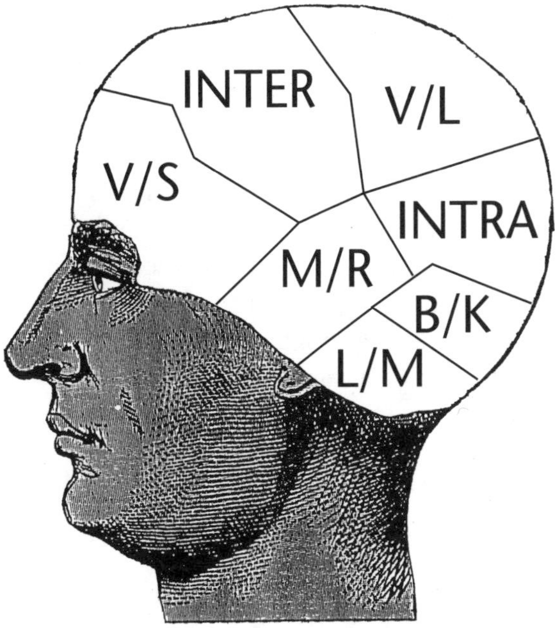

Figure 1.2

Intelligence Is the Ability to Creatively Problem Solve

We as humans can invent and discover. We are always thinking of a new way, a different angle. When children are given a set of manipulatives to explore and create, they are creating, or problem solving, by moving from chaos to structure. They are creating a formation from randomness. As adults, we are doing the same thing anytime we come up with a new way to do something or create a different use for a tool or gadget.

Intelligence Is the Ability to Contribute to One's Cultural Setting

An individual must be able to use his or her intelligence to create and solve problems that are appropriate to his or her cultural setting. The ability to recognize and name twenty different kinds of snow is merely an intellectual exercise to a banker in southern Florida, but significant information to a geologist in northern Alaska. The contributions of artists, inventors, musicians, athletes, writers, and explorers from around the globe have made the world a better place for us all.

■ Gardner's Multiple Intelligences

There were many candidates for "intelligences" that met Gardner's definition. However, after testing numerous criteria, only seven intelligences remained (Gardner 1983). Each of us have at least seven intelligences. In Carolyn Chapman's *If the Shoe Fits . . . : How to Develop Multiple Intelligences in the Classroom*, the seven intelligences are defined as follows (see also fig. 1.3).

Verbal/Linguistic Intelligence

The verbal/linguistic intelligence is language related. It involves the ability to read, write, listen, speak, and link information. People with this intelligence are sensitive to the meanings of words and their manipulation, formation, and selection. These individuals are aware of the varying functions of language or, more specifically, of its power to stimulate emotions. Poets, authors, reporters, speakers, teachers, attorneys, talk-show hosts, and politicians typically exhibit strengths in the verbal/linguistic intelligence. This intelligence is emphasized in today's schools, helping to foster a literate America.

Musical/Rhythmic Intelligence

As Gardner (1983) describes, "There are several roles that musically inclined individuals can assume, ranging from the avant-garde composer who attempts to create a new idiom, to the fledgling listener who is trying to make sense of nursery rhymes (or other 'primer level' music)" (p. 104). Each of us holds musical capabilities to some degree; the difference is that some people have more skill than others. No matter how talented we are, we all use core abilities to enjoy music. These include the musical elements of pitch, rhythm, and timbre (the characteristic elements of a tone). The musical/rhythmic intelligence is the auditory learner in us all. The sounds of our world, environmental and musical, and one's awareness, enjoyment, and use of these sounds make up this intelligence. People with a more highly developed musical/rhythmic intelligence are singers, composers, instrumentalists, conductors, and those who enjoy, understand, or appreciate music.

The Multiple Intelligences

	Intelligence	Shoe	Reason for the Shoe	Key Component of the Intelligence
Language Related	Verbal/ Linguistic		The tap shoe, the communicating shoe, represents the verbal/linguistic learner. The shoe makes the tapping sounds that tell us the message of the dancer. This symbolizes interpretation. When the dancer moves to the beat and taps out every sound, we interpret the full message.	• reading • listening • writing • speaking • linking and transfering of information
	Musical/ Rhythmic		The drum major's boot is worn as the leader of the beat marches in front of the band. Counting the time with his baton, he keeps the band in rhythm as it plays a harmonious tune. He is aware of the sound and the beat; the beat-mind connection.	• auditory learning • music • pitch, tone, inflection, rhythm, timbre • awareness of environmental sounds • musical instruments
Object Related	Logical/ Mathematical		The hiking boot symbolizes the pattern seeker as represented by the laces. The problem-solving and critical-thinking hiker climbs step by step up the challenging path. This is the tough shoe of the abstract thinker.	• numbers • critical thinking • abstract, inductive, deductive reasoning • patterns • technology and gadgets • research and data gathering
	Visual/ Spatial		Cinderella's glass slipper represents the world of imagination and creativity. The images in the glass symbolize the images one sees behind one's eyelids. The way one sees the world in the "mind's eye" is that personal view of the world as pictured in one's mind.	• creativity, fantasy, imagination • colors • art media of all types • spatial relationships • abstract thinking
	Bodily/ Kinesthetic		What shoe could possibly represent the bodily/kinesthetic learner better than the athletic shoe? The wearer is a picture of grace and skill in movement, using the body to express thoughts, actions, and emotions. Those wearing the sports-minded shoe are proactive learners—the doers.	• sports and fitness • manipulatives • action • body relationships to the outside world • tactile
Person Related	Intrapersonal		The warm, comfortable bedroom slipper represents one's time to learn about one's self in a quiet, cozy, peaceful spot of one's own choosing. One who wears this shoe enjoys time alone, feels peace, and can identify goals, strengths, and areas to improve.	• self-knowledge • reflection • metacognition • journals • self-talk • goal setting • decision making
	Interpersonal		The football cleats represent the teaming of the interpersonal intelligence. Each member must do his of her part to make the team plays. Working for and with others is one of the goals.	• team player • social actions and skills • getting along with others • dependent learner

Figure 1.3

IRI/Skylight Training and Publishing, Inc.

Logical/Mathematical Intelligence

The logical/mathematical intelligence incorporates both mathematical and scientific abilities. Mathematicians are typically characterized by an enjoyment of working with abstraction and a desire for exploration. They enjoy working with problems that require a great deal of reasoning. Scientists, however, are characterized by a desire to explain physical reality. For scientists, mathematics serves as a tool for building models and theories. Mathematicians, engineers, physicists, astronomers, computer programmers, and researchers demonstrate a high degree of logical/mathematical intelligence.

Visual/Spatial Intelligence

Visual/spatial intelligence involves the unique ability to accurately comprehend the visual world. Those with visual/spatial intelligence are able to represent spatial information graphically and have a keen gift for bringing forth and transforming mental images. Artists and designers have strong visual/spatial capabilities. They have a certain responsiveness to the visual/spatial world as well as a talent to re-create this world as a work of art. Also among this group are sailors, engineers, surgeons, sculptors, cartographers, and architects.

Bodily/Kinesthetic Intelligence

The bodily/kinesthetic intelligence is based on the ability to control one's bodily motions and the talent to manipulate objects with deftness. Individuals with a strength in this intelligence interact with their environment through touch and movement and often have a highly developed sense of direction. People such as inventors and actors tend to have a great deal of bodily/kinesthetic intelligence; the role of their bodies is critical to their occupations. Others with substantial bodily/kinesthetic intelligence include dancers, acrobats, and athletes.

Intrapersonal Intelligence

The heart of the intrapersonal intelligence lies in the ability to understand one's own feelings. People with a strong intrapersonal intelligence instinctively comprehend their own range of emotions, label them, and draw on them as a means of directing their own behavior. In Gardner's words, "the intrapersonal intelligence amounts to little more than the capacity to distinguish a feeling of pleasure from one of pain, and on the basis of such discrimination, to become more involved in or to withdraw from a situation" (1983, 239). Examples of those with higher-than-average intrapersonal capabilities include the introspective novelist, wise elder, psychologist, or therapist—all of whom possess a deep understanding of their feelings.

Interpersonal Intelligence

Unlike intrapersonal intelligence, which is directed inward, interpersonal intelligence focuses outward toward individuals in the environment. The most basic skill among those with a high degree of interpersonal intelligence is the talent for understanding others. Those exhibiting this intelligence notice and make distinctions among other individuals, and more specifically, about their "moods, temperaments, motivations, and intentions" (Gardner 1983, 239). For example, at a very simple level, this intelligence includes the ability of a child to notice and be sensitive to the moods of adults around him or her. A more complex interpersonal skill is the ability of adults to read the intentions of others, even when hidden. People exhibiting this intelligence include religious and political leaders, parents, teachers, therapists, and counselors.

■ Multiple Intelligences with Centers and Projects

Today's classrooms must meet students' individual needs. To do this, educators must create classrooms that are mind centered instead of content centered. Curricula that are hands on and require students to work in centers or on projects target a specific intelligence. Tasks become more challenging, lively, and thought provoking, and students become proactive in their decision making and problem solving. Most importantly, when students work at a center or on a project, the *process* becomes as important as the *product*.

Centers, which allow students to discover in an exploratory or a structured setting, and projects, which involve students in studying a content-related subject that results in a product, give students opportunities to make choices. Students plan their learning activities, set goals, and determine how they will present what they have learned. Centers and projects also provide students with the opportunity to learn through all of their intelligences—to identify and enhance their strengths and to develop their areas of weakness. As students utilize centers and projects and begin to understand and apply their intelligences and their thinking processes, they become effective decision makers, problem solvers, and lifelong learners.

About Centers

Centers provide students with hands-on, in-class experiences to practice, reteach, discover, enrich, and enhance learning. Students work on activities that engage all of their intelligences to help them learn content and develop thinking and problem-solving skills. Working both independently and in small groups, students experience a natural integration of intelligences when they are engaged in accomplishing tasks at learning centers.

Center activities teach the process of planning when students select and organize their tasks. When students are responsible for their learning, they strive not only to fulfill their potential but also to push beyond their own expectations of themselves. Students take pride in the products they create at the centers because they have the opportunity to interject individuality into their work. Teachers, too, find their expectations and understanding of each student's potential heightened as they guide the learning process.

Centers provide students with opportunities to learn and explore content through a variety of manipulatives and intelligences. They also help students develop social and thinking skills (see fig. 2.1). Centers do more than provide pencil-and-paper exercise that engages only one or two intelligences and provides little opportunity for interaction or thinking-skill development. Centers stimulate all of a student's intelligences and encourage the development of skills for lifelong learning.

Skills Developed through Learning Centers	
Social Skills	**Thinking Skills**
1. responsibility	1. synthesizing
2. following directions, rules, and procedures	2. processing
3. working independently and cooperatively	3. problem solving
4. pride in work	4. using available resources
5. goal setting	5. sequencing
6. on-task behavior	6. predicting
7. commitment	7. analyzing
8. listening	8. decision making
9. respect for others	9. data gathering
10. acceptance of others	10. imagining

Figure 2.1

■ *Creating Centers*

In designing learning centers one must consider both environmental and instructional factors. Finding a physical location in the classroom for each center is an appropriate place to start. Students will need adequate space to work and a surface that is sufficient for the task. For instance, a visual/spatial center can provide a large, flat surface, such as a table, for students to sit at and draw, paint, sculpt, etc. A bodily/kinesthetic center, however, might be best equipped with a sand table or simply a large, empty space for movement activities. Each center should be located in an area of the room where students can work comfortably and effectively with the least amount of noise disturbance to or from students involved in centers or projects in other parts of the room.

Instruction is the other consideration in designing centers. The teacher must first decide if a center is an exploratory center or a structured center. In either case, the center must have a significant purpose (see figs. 2.2–2.5). Students should not visit centers to do busywork. If a center is structured, the activities or the tasks must be determined. The teacher needs to decide how directions will be presented at each center and whether students will work on tasks individually or cooperatively.

How to Begin

1. **Decide how many centers to create.** A center-based classroom works most effectively when there are enough centers for all students to have a place to work simultaneously. At some centers, students will work independently. At others, they will work in small groups of two to five students. When students are working independently, more than one student can be at

Brainstorming Ideas for Exploratory or Structured Centers

Unit of focus: _____

Verbal/Linguistic:	Musical/Rhythmic:
Logical/Mathematical:	Visual/Spatial:
Bodily/Kinesthetic:	Intrapersonal:
Interpersonal:	Arrangement Tips:

Figure 2.2

IRI/Skylight Training and Publishing, Inc.

Designing Your Own Center Time

Figure 2.3

My Plan

Purposes/goals for center time:

Length of time:

When? How often?

Management plan for center time:

Figure 2.4

Centers for Implementation: The Plan

Unit of focus: _____

Targeted Intelligence: **Materials:** **Task:**	**Targeted Intelligence:** **Materials:** **Task:**
Targeted Intelligence: **Materials:** **Task:**	**Targeted Intelligence:** **Materials:** **Task:**
Targeted Intelligence: **Materials:** **Task:**	**Targeted Intelligence:** **Materials:** **Task:**
Targeted Intelligence: **Materials:** **Task:**	**Targeted Intelligence:** **Materials:** **Task:**

Figure 2.5

IRI/Skylight Training and Publishing, Inc.

the center at the same time; however, all students must have easy access to the materials, and there must be enough materials and supplies to accommodate the chosen number of students at each center.

2. **Determine the instructional focus.** Whether exploratory or structured, multiple intelligences centers can (1) reflect what is currently being taught in the curricula, (2) review information, or (3) explore upcoming topics. Center-based classrooms should have centers that cover all of these instructional focuses.

3. **Assess available materials and resources.** Consider the materials and resources you have available in your classroom. Even basic household items make good manipulatives. Be creative.

4. **Choose a name for each center.** Some teachers name centers after famous people or places. Others choose common names that students can easily identify. You can establish names for the entire year or change them each semester or quarter. Students often enjoy helping choose the names.

5. **Decide how long center time will be.** On the average, students should spend twenty-five to thirty minutes at each center. Depending on how you choose to structure the day, students can rotate through several centers in one day or over the course of a week. By having a specific time set aside for center activities, students will know what to expect and will be prepared for the transition.

6. **Establish rules for center time.** Rules help guarantee successful centers (see fig. 2.6). Involve students in determining the rules. Be sure to consider all aspects, such as movement from center to center, respect for materials and others' workspace, retrieving and cleaning up materials, and noise level. Once rules have been established, stick to them.

7. **Set up a procedure for getting students into centers.** Even if students know when center time is scheduled each day or week, they need guidance for moving into the appropriate centers. Students should know which center they are assigned to—or should be given instructions on how to choose a center—and when and how to move to that center when it's time.

How to Set Up the Room

As mentioned earlier, noise is an important consideration in setting up centers. Whenever possible, put quiet centers together and put noisier, more active centers in more remote parts of the room. Use tables, desktops, areas on the floor or rug, easels, chalkboards, and space under tables for work areas. A designated workspace for each center is essential (see fig. 2.7).

Cards or signs can be used to label each center with its chosen name. Students can work in small groups at the visual/spatial center and create these labels.

Rules for Center Time

Getting materials out:

Signals for attention:

Choosing a center:

Changing centers:

Displaying materials:

Noise-level controls:

Time out:

Clean up/returning materials:

Figure 2.6

Room Layout: The Plan

Figure 2.7

■ Types of Centers

Exploratory Centers

Material and workspace is assigned in an exploratory center; however, it is the individual's responsibility to create, discover, invent, manipulate, and/or explore the process and product. The student makes choices, solves problems, creates problems, makes decisions, and learns what the manipulatives can do—all of which are an important part of discovery for the thinking mind.

The main focus of all centers should be the processes and the products the students develop. By asking students for certain information in journals, logs, or conferences, the teacher can discover the students' step-by-step thinking processes. The following questions guide the student to think and process with reflection:

1. How did you do this?
2. Tell me about what you are doing.
3. What were you thinking as you did this?
4. Why did you do this?
5. Is there anything you would change?
6. What are you going to do next?

Structured Centers

In structured centers, the management rules are set, the workspace is provided, and the objectives and procedures of the task are explained. Structured center activities give learners the opportunity to work through the application of a concept and independently practice a skill.

Example: Practicing a Skill

1. Vocabulary is taught at the writing center by providing students with cards, some with vocabulary words on them and others with the definition of those words. Students must match the words to their definition.
2. At the games center, students practice following directions and rules.

Example: Adding to a Skill

1. Students solve problems on skill cards at the math center; then, they make up new problems on skill cards for others to solve.

2. Students in the music center are shown whole notes and half notes and practice different rhythms with small instruments; then for example, by understanding tempo, students can determine the length of a quarter note.

■ Moving Into and Out of Centers

Assigning Centers

A clothespin chart (fig. 2.8) is a creative, visual way to assign students to centers. First, divide a large piece of paper into sections according to the number of centers there are. Write the names of the centers in the sections. Decide how many children can comfortably work at each center at one time. Clip clothespins to each labeled square to represent the number of students that will be working at each center. Color-coded clothespins make the chart easier to follow. Label locations/work stations in the room with colored signs to match the clothespins.

Designate and name five or six groups of students in the room. Students can be divided by rows or table or by their cooperative base groups. Allow the groups some choice over the center they visit. For example, the groups could be named Monday, Tuesday, Wednesday, Thursday, and Friday. On Monday, the Monday group would choose their center first, followed by the Tuesday group, the Wednesday group, etc. On Tuesday, the Tuesday group would choose first, followed by the Wednesday group, etc., and the Monday group would go last. This gives each group one day to choose their favorite center.

Assigning groups to centers is another option. However, most teachers find that students take more responsibility for their learning when they have participated in the decision-making process. Also, teachers can learn a lot about individual students by observing which centers they prefer and which centers they ignore or avoid.

However, at certain times there will be a center that all the students need to visit during the week to complete a project or practice a skill. In this case, the first group can be assigned to this center while the remaining groups continue to choose a center, following the procedure above. For example, on Monday, the Monday group would be assigned to the art center, then the Tuesday would group choose their center, followed by the Wednesday group, etc. On Tuesday, the Tuesday group would go to the art center, then the Wednesday group chooses their center, and so on. This process would be followed until all have finished the project in the art center.

Circulating Students

There are several ways to have students circulate from group to group. If there is a clothespin available on the board, the learner may go and swap his or her clothespin for the available one and move to the new center. The student is responsible for choosing where to move next. However, the teacher establishes the guidelines for swapping, including whether or not the

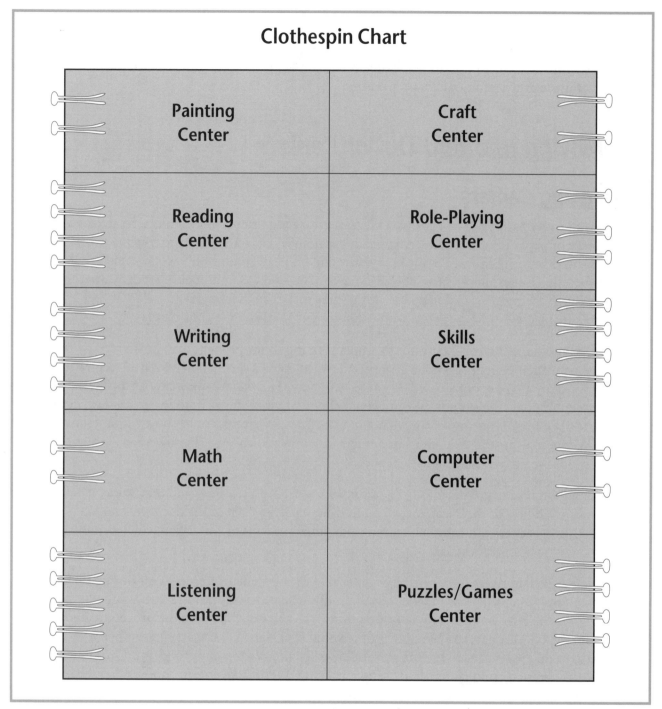

Clothespin Chart

Painting Center	Craft Center
Reading Center	Role-Playing Center
Writing Center	Skills Center
Math Center	Computer Center
Listening Center	Puzzles/Games Center

Figure 2.8

Instructions
1. Write in the boxes the names of the centers you are setting up.
2. Think about how many children can comfortably use each center at a time.
3. Put clothespins on the chart to represent that number at each center.
4. Color code the clothespins to correspond to each of the different centers you have set up.
5. Label locations/workstations in the room. You may want to color-code them to match the clothespins.

students must finish the task they are working on at one center before moving to another. Using this procedure, a teacher can observe students' attention spans, movement, frustrations, areas of concentration, favorite centers, and avoided centers.

Another way to move students to a different center is to have the student explain to the teacher why he or she is ready to move to another center before swapping his or her clothespin. Students are still responsible for their decision to move to another center, but now they must explain why they want to move.

Changing Centers

If few students choose a particular center, something is wrong with the center, not with the students. It needs to be altered, "hammed up," or eliminated entirely. If the objective, concept, or skill the center teaches is important, think of another way to make it more interesting and appealing. A center should also be changed or eliminated if there are too many centers that focus on the same skill or intelligence. Getting into a rut does not foster quality use of time.

If the activities at a center are too easy and require little thinking, they become busywork and are not an effective use of center time. Add challenge to or change a center that doesn't foster enough quality thinking, creativity, or problem solving.

Sometimes a center might need to be moved to another area of the room because of noise levels, space, or availability of materials interfere with learning. Also, once activities in centers are underway, the teacher may find that the number of students working at a particular center at any one time will need to be altered because of the workspace required.

Keeping Centers

A center that is successful and worth keeping is one that is frequently visited. A center is valuable if it helps students learn a concept, objective, or skill that they need to practice or supports the classroom curriculum. The final criterion of a successful center is that it challenges students and encourages their creativity, thinking and problem-solving skills.

■ Establishing Rules and Guidelines

Any time a new center is created in a classroom, the students must be told how to do the activities (if there are specific activities). They must know what the expectations and rules are for that particular center and its materials. It helps if teachers can role-play the directions and rules with the students.

Directions

Establish a color-coded direction system. For example, step one is green, step two is orange, step three is blue, step four is red, etc. This way students know that after they do the green step, the orange step is next, and so on. Consistency helps establish order and sequence in following directions.

Workspace

Be sure a specific place or surface is indicated for working on the activity. If a manipulative is being used, the back of a carpet square or a cookie sheet often works well. For activities that require a lot of space, specify a work area such as an area rug, table, or space on the floor.

Use and Storage of Materials

Let students know the specific materials that they need for each activity or that are available for exploring. If they are using class materials and resources such as books, tapes, or equipment, establish rules for their proper use and care.

Sometimes students will need a place to store their materials and display their completed products. Designating a spot under a table or in an isolated area of the classroom is one alternative for storing projects and/or materials. This will prevent problems of stepping on or around them. Hanging completed artifacts on a clothesline is a handy, manageable way to organize and show off center work.

Remind students that everything has a home. If they use materials, they must put them back in their proper place when they are finished. Students should know that they need to clean up their workspace before they leave a center, leaving it cleaner than when they began.

Noise Level

Buzzing noise is constructive noise! Part of the problem-solving process will involve noise. However, disruptive, off-task noise should be controlled. Establish the fact that it is a privilege to work at a center. If a student does not comply with the noise guidelines, he or she should take a time-out for disruptive behavior.

Discipline Tips

The following techniques are suggestions for disciplining students when using centers. The main rule is to be consistent, no matter which method you establish.

Verbal Reprimand

First, tell the student the specific inappropriate behavior you observed. Then, tell the student what behavior you expected to see. In order to return to the center, the student must tell you what he or she did wrong and how the behavior can be changed to remedy the situation.

Open/Closed Signs

If a center is not being used properly, it may need to be closed for a period of time. One way to do this is to create an open/closed sign for each center and turn the sign to read "closed" on the center in question. If students are in the center at the time, they must return their clothespins to the board and quietly proceed to another center. Before opening the center again, have a class discussion to reestablish the working rules for this space.

Red/Yellow/Green Light Boards

In order to monitor the noise level in the classroom at center time, create a red/yellow/green light board. This board, designed to look like a traffic light, will indicate to the students the teacher's interpretation of the noise level in the classroom. At the beginning of center time, clip a clothespin to the green light. If the noise level rises to an uncomfortable level, caution the class by moving the clothespin to the yellow light. If the students know that the clothespin on red means center time will be discontinued, they will quickly quiet down when it is on yellow so that the teacher can move it back to green.

Background Music

Listening to instrumental music during center time is a privilege most students enjoy. Music, however, is also an effective way to monitor the noise level in the classroom. If the students can no longer hear the music, they will know that they are being too noisy.

Remember, if a center is constructive, encourages processing, has clear ground rules, and easy-to-use, accessible materials, students will be excited about working there.

■ Assessing Center Time

If centers are not planned properly, they can be a waste of time. If students simply play with manipulatives without processing their play, it is not profitable to their learning. However, when students talk about their actions, they develop the attributes of critical and creative thinkers.

When students cease to challenge their minds, and do the same things repeatedly, boredom sets in. This indicates that it is time for a change. Teachers can walk from center to center and find out what students are doing and learning during center time. Teachers can use the gathered data to make curriculum decisions (e.g., What do the students need next?).

Conferencing

When conferencing with a student during center time, look at the material from the student's perspective. Make eye contact with the student and ask questions about the work and his or her thinking process. Open-ended statements that encourage students to talk about what they are thinking and doing are also effective. For example, a teacher could say, "Tell me about what you are doing"; "Tell me what you were thinking about when you did this"; "Tell me how you did this"; or "Read that to me."

When students are questioned, they usually think they have done something wrong. For best conferencing results, listen as the students talk through their thinking, step by step, explaining a problem they solved or something they created. Many times the teacher will have to say: "Tell me how you figured out the answer for number three. It's the right answer, so don't change it. Tell me how you got that answer or came to that conclusion." Then the student can explain what he or she knows. Too many times teachers give students information they already have and could be sharing themselves.

If students tend to focus on their mistakes or don't think they have answered problems the right way, teachers can show students that there are many ways to solve a problem. In addition, other students can explain the process they used to get an answer or ask leading questions to guide another student through his or her thinking.

A teacher who uses centers told us that after using center time for one hour a day throughout the school year, she knew more about her students and what they knew than any other year she had ever taught. She attributed her success to the effective questioning and conferencing she used during center time. Mediating for information can help determine the necessary total group instruction, reteaching, enhancement, and enrichment (see fig. 2.9). It also guides the teacher in knowing what centers to keep, revamp, or replace.

Student Self-Assessment of Centers

While conferencing is done during center time, student self-assessment occurs after an activity has been completed. Self-assessment allows students to reflect on their activities at a center as well as on the center itself.

Journals/Logs

Students can record reflections about their work during center time in journals or logs. Make sure that the students date their work and record which centers they are speaking of in their entry.

Conferencing/Assessment

Teacher:

Students:

Peers:

Figure 2.9

IRI/Skylight Training and Publishing, Inc.

Feedback Graffiti Board

Locate a spot such as a bulletin board, the side of a filing cabinet, or a wall section for students to write their "Center News." Post a large sheet of paper for students to write reflections or discoveries made during center times.

Class Graphs

Make a list of the current classroom centers. Have students vote on their favorite center. This will reveal the students' likes and dislikes. An unpopular center needs to be revamped or replaced.

Feedback

Each student can be given a Likert scale (see fig. 2.10) drawn on paper or a card. Students draw a mark on the scale for each center they visited that day or week reflecting their level of comfort or discomfort with the center. Students can label the marks so the teacher can see which center each mark corresponds to. Different colors can be used to make it easier to read the chart.

Students can also draw faces that illustrate how they feel about working at each center. The mouths and expressions on the faces should indicate the students' likes and dislikes (see fig. 2.11).

Two other forms of quick feedback are the Color Box and the AHA! Box. In the first, students divide a piece of paper into two sections and label it with the name of a center they worked at that day or week. They can then color a section of the paper with a color that symbolizes how they felt when they were working at that center. The student can then write why they felt that way in the other section (see fig. 2.12).

In the AHA! Box, students reflect on the center they worked at that day or that week and record in the box the name of the center and the most important thing they learned while working at it (see fig. 2.13).

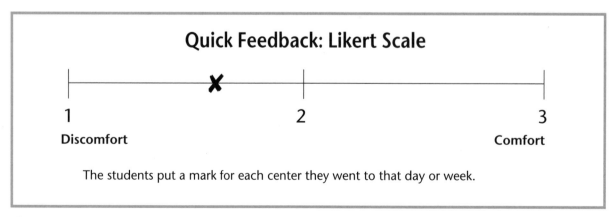

Figure 2.10

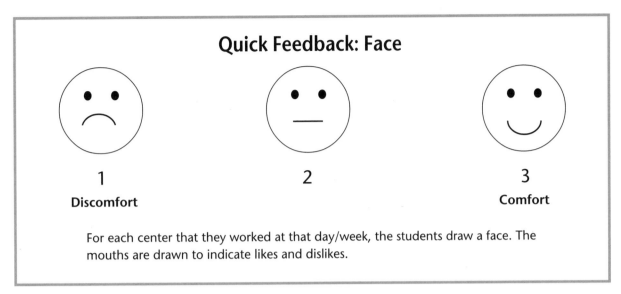

Figure 2.11

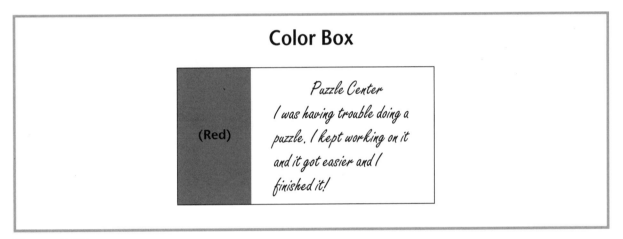

Figure 2.12

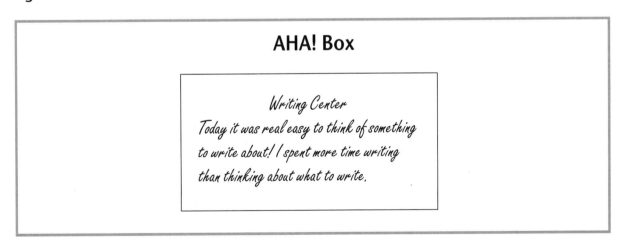

Figure 2.13

CHAPTER 3

Exploratory Centers

Exploratory centers can lead students into a state of flow—a state where the mind is challenged and engaged (Csikszentmihalyi 1990). They provide time for students to make choices, be creative, solve problems, and strengthen their intelligences. Dendrites—branching processes of a neuron that conduct impulses toward the cell body—grow in our brain when the mind is challenged. When exploratory center times are effective, learners grow dendrites. In other words, they "grow brain."

In exploratory centers, students decide what they are going to do and how they will accomplish tasks. The open-endedness of these centers allows students to explore, create, discover, and problem solve. These actions create thinking and inquiring minds. It should be emphasized, however, that in order to maximize the learning potential of exploratory centers, a teacher must constantly move through them, encouraging students to reflect on their activities.

Once the teacher and students have mastered exploratory centers, he or she will be ready to engage in centers, both stuctured and exploratory, that are linked to units of study such as those presented in Section Two.

Following are suggestions for exploratory centers for multiple intelligences (see also fig. 3.1).

Suggested Props for Centers for Each of the Intelligences

Verbal/ Linguistic	Musical/ Rhythmic	Logical/ Mathematical	Visual/ Spatial	Bodily/ Kinesthetic	Intra- personal	Inter- personal
• reading lamp • pillows • stuffed animals • various sizes, shapes, textures of paper • variety of writing implements • variety of reading materials	• records, tapes, CDs • listening center • tape recorder • record player • CD player • instruments • objects that make noise • nature sounds • sticks • drums • bells	• puzzles • games • brain teasers • task cards • graphing paper • calendar • time lines • clocks • calculators • computers • counters • measuring devices	• junk box • murals • easels • paints • markers • chalk • crayons • charcoal • clay • paper of different sizes, shapes, textures • camera • transparen- cies • buttons • videos, filmstrips • popsicle sticks • illustrations • display area • posters, charts, pictures	• manipul- atives • overhead projector • counters • blocks • sports equipment • labs • collections • sand tables • water tables	• journals • logs • goal cards • "All About Me" books • biographies • time lines of life • photo albums • autobiogra- phies	• team games • think-pair- share • jigsaw • shared drawings • group puzzles, brain teasers • computers with e-mail

Figure 3.1

■ Verbal/Linguistic

Writing Center

Successful writing centers have paper of all sizes, shapes, colors, and textures and a variety of writing instruments, including different types of pens and pencils, markers, and chalk. Additional useful materials include word banks, dictionaries, thesauruses, and other reference books.

If computers are available, students can use word-processing software to type in favorite pieces. A printer would provide an opportunity for learners to see their work as a product.

A fun addition to the writing center is a visor with captions such as "writer," "editor," "writing staff," "I am a writer," or "I can write." Put up a sign at the center that says "Writing in Progress," "Writing Zone," or "Editor's Corner."

Reading Center

The reading center should be a comfortable nook for independent reading. Provide a variety of comfortable places for students to sit—a rug, carpet squares, pillows, beanbags, rocking chair, a table and chairs. Allow students to choose a spot in this center that suits them. Add a reading lamp to give the center a cozy, comfortable, at-home feeling.

The center should be supplied with age-appropriate reading materials that interest the students. Display a variety of fiction and nonfiction. Include class-made books, team-written books, and individual pieces if they are available. Many students enjoy reading works by authors they know.

Consider using signs for this center such as "Reading Is Fun," "Reading in Progress," "Busy-Bee Readers," "Cool Readers," and "The Reader's Nook."

Listening Center

Listening centers should provide a variety of stories, songs, poems, and other favorites for students to enjoy. Some stories available on audiotape often include a book or other material for the listener to follow. The teacher can also tape record students' favorite stories, which they can then follow along in the book. To indicate that it is time to turn the page in a taped story, use a sound that corresponds to the setting of the story. For example, in travel stories, use an engine or horn sound; in farm stories, use an animal sound. Always use the same sound throughout the book and explain the directions before the story begins. All self-made tapes should include the names of the author and the illustrator or the composer at the beginning of the tape. If students do not have books or materials to follow along with, have them draw or sculpt with clay. When tapes of songs are played, students can sing along.

Speaking Center

In this center, students can record their favorite stories, poems, songs, or creative writing pieces, or they can read them to a partner. Students can also use time at this center to record themselves talking about things of interest, or they can record their reflections about learning.

Another speaking center activity is to have one student give another student directions, such as how to fold a paper airplane or make a peanut butter-and-jelly sandwich. Using manipulatives, one student can explain to another how to organize the pieces to create a picture or a figure. When the task is completed, the partners can discuss why the directions did or didn't work and what would have made the process easier.

■ Visual/Spatial

Painting Center

Include a variety of brushes and colors of paints at this center. Large men's shirts or paint smocks are recommended to keep spills and splatters off the students' clothes. Store the paints in nonspill containers for less mess.

Ideally, a painting center should be equipped with easels. For young children, set up an easel in a plastic swimming pool large enough for the painter and easel. Messes will land in the pool and will be easier to clean up. For older children, drop cloths or plastic tablecloths under an easel help contain messes. Two-, three-, or four-sided easels can be built or purchased for classroom use.

Teachers can supply colored markers at the easels instead of paints. Markers work well with a variety of sizes of paper, from note cards to murals. Store markers in cans with the writing tips facing the bottom of the can so the ink drains toward the tip.

A fun part of painting is displaying the work. Hang a string near the painting center and use clothespins or paper clips for drying, storing, and displaying.

Junk Box Center

In this center, students can work at tables to create works of art from "junk." Stock the center with a variety of materials such as fabric scraps, small cardboard boxes, buttons, yarn, and string, as well as glue, paste, tape, scissors, and paper (see appendix A for additional suggestions). Encourage students to be creative. You may want to make suggestions of things they could make, such as sculptures, collages, hats, banners, flags, bookcovers, and mobiles.

Projection Center

Set up an overhead projector either on a table or on the floor so that the light projects onto one of the center's bare walls. Create transparencies for students to view on the overhead, such as diagrams, maps, and drawings. Allow students to create their own overheads using blank transparencies, then view the results on the wall.

■ Bodily/Kinesthetic

Practice Centers

Practicing spelling, cursive writing, and math problems becomes tedious and boring for students who only practice on paper. Younger students particularly like to move around and touch things. The following are some creative ideas to satisfy students' desires to "get their hands into things," and to get them to practice the fundamentals.

Gel Bags

Collect several sealable freezer bags (e.g., Ziploc bags). Put enough hair gel in each bag to cover the surface area of the bag when it is sealed and lying on its side (about $1/4$ filled). Reinforce the sealed bags with packaging or heavy black tape. Instruct students to use the tip of their finger, not their fingernail, to write on the bag. This activity is great for practicing letters, spelling, or numbers.

Salt Trays

Collect several Styrofoam meat trays. Cover the bottom of the trays with salt. Students can use their fingers to practice cursive writing or spelling.

Magic Slates

Students who like using chalk will enjoy writing on their own chalkboard. Secure two pieces of string to a small chalkboard and attach a piece of chalk to one and a sock (as an eraser) to the other. Students can practice writing or math problems.

Magnetic Letters and Numbers

Gather a variety of magnetic letters and numbers in different colors for students to practice with. Magnetic surfaces can be created with magnetic tape, or students can use the sides of filing cabinets, desks, or cookie sheets.

Manipulative Discovery Center

Make manipulatives available for students to explore, discover, and create. Teachers are often told to keep the play out of the manipulative, but it is important for students to discover and explore manipulatives. By doing so, learners are aware of what they are doing and can talk about their thinking process. This is a step toward self-reflection, or metacognition.

Dyed Materials

Rice or variously shaped noodles can safely and easily be dyed in different colors. To dye, add four tablespoons of food coloring and two tablespoons of rubbing alcohol to a large Ziploc freezer bag. Add rice or noodles and shake until covered. Continue adding rice or noodles until all the liquid is absorbed. Spread rice or noodles on waxed paper to dry. Put dyed materials in the center for students to use to explore concepts such as measuring and conservation. A large container, bucket, galvanized tub, plastic swimming pool, or waste table is ideal for storing these materials.

Craft Materials

Junk boxes (see appendix A), collage materials, paints, clay, scissors, glue, and seasonal objects for crafts can be placed at this center for students eager to discover and create. Some activity examples are seasonal crafts, woodworking, and sculptures.

Sculpting Materials

Creating three-dimensional designs with sculpting materials is as important in art centers as creating flat-surface art. Students can use manipulatives such as clay, papier-mâché, wire coat hangers, paper towels, tissue-paper rolls, boxes, etc., to sculpt their works of art.

Costume Center

This center is excellent for role playing. Collect all kinds of hats, shoes, jewelry, capes, costumes, and other articles of clothing to create a dress-up center. A mirror, as well as props such as umbrellas, suitcases, briefcases, and lunchboxes will make this area even more fun. Students can create a cast of characters to act out a story or set up a room or scene such as one of the following:

House: supply tables, chairs, play stove and refrigerator, tea set, dolls, aprons, dishpans, silverware, plastic glasses, pitchers, etc.

Post Office: supply envelopes, paper, rubber stamps, writing implements, cash register, mailbox.

Grocery Store: supply paper for grocery list, empty food containers and boxes, plastic vegetables and fruit, cash register, grocery bags.

■ Logical/Mathematical

Critical-Thinking Center

A critical-thinking center can contain brain teasers, word and number puzzles, a problem of the day/week, and any other challenging problems for students to solve. This center can be set up with a table or desks and chairs, or students can stand at the chalkboard.

Puzzle Center

Collect both wooden and cardboard puzzles for this center. Set up students in a convenient workplace, such as under a table or in a corner of the room. In this way, students can continue working on a more difficult puzzle over the course of several visits to the center rather than beginning again each time.

You can also create your own puzzles (or have students create them). Find a large picture of something the students are studying, mount it on cardboard, and laminate it. Cut it into puzzle pieces and store the pieces in a Ziploc bag.

Pattern Center

A pattern center should include counters of various shapes, colors, and/or textures, such as dried beans, noodles, and building blocks. Ample workspace must be provided for the students to explore patterns, such as a straight line, stair steps, or a spiral.

Math Manipulative Center

Any object that serves as a math manipulative for counting can be used at this center. For example, pattern blocks, Unifix cubes, Cuissinaire rods, and small objects for sorting and counting can be explored. This is a good place for students to create their own problems to solve.

Construction Center

Possible items to include at this center are a drafting table with paper and materials, wood, Legos, boxes of all sizes, construction sets of all kinds, blocks, and toothpicks. Students can design and build structures or construct objects using these materials.

Measuring Center

This center should be stocked with various measuring devices such as compasses, rulers, yardsticks, tape measures, protractors, balance scales, measuring cups, and containers of all sizes and shapes. Students will need items that they can measure such as dried beans, rice, or objects from around the room.

■ Musical/Rhythmic

Listening Center

Depending on the music equipment available, include in this center materials such as records, tapes, or CDs of different types of music by different artists.

If students are going to listen to different pieces at the same time, headphones will be necessary. Students can use paper and writing instruments to interpret the sounds or the mood set by the music and its tempo.

Recording Center

Cassette recorders can be used to record students' songs, chants, cheers, raps, choral readings, or poems. These recordings can include class compositions, individuals' compositions, or students' favorites.

Music Software Center

If computers and music software are available, let the students enjoy learning and practicing rhythms, notes, and composition. Students can use these programs to study the composition and notation of a tune they already know, or they can compose new verses, tunes, or rhythmic patterns.

Instrument Center

Make a variety of musical instruments such as keyboards, tambourines, drums, and triangles available in this center. Students can also create their own instruments, such as beanbags, shakers, and rhythm sticks.

Students can explore the sounds and purposes of the different instruments and experiment with their own musical talent. Some center groups may want to form a small band and work on playing a tune together. Others may want to listen to a recording of a song and then choose instruments to play along.

Encourage students to create songs, poems, raps, chants, cheers, and jingles of their own. Make a tape recorder available for students to record their compositions.

■ Interpersonal

Any center which accommodates more than one student at one time can focus on the interpersonal intelligence. Ideal working groups are made up of two, three, and four students. Be sure the students have enough physical space to facilitate small group work. The following center activities focus on the interpersonal intelligence.

Group Games and Puzzles

Store classroom games and puzzles in cabinets, on shelves, or in tubs. Groups should choose a game or puzzle and work together to play or solve it. Post lists of social skills and center rules where groups can see them, and be sure they are followed.

If there are only a limited number of games and puzzles, invite volunteers, teachers, other school personnel, and parents to a game shower; everyone can bring a game or a puzzle to donate to the centers at the school. The games and puzzles can be housed in the media center for school use, and teachers can check them out as needed for the centers.

Group Problems

At centers where manipulatives, props, or story-problem task cards are being used, students can work in groups to think through problems, process, and reach consensus.

Group Exploration

Again, using manipulatives, students can explore in groups by deciding on a plan, carrying out the plan, and discussing the plan as they create a product. For example, a small group of students can construct a building or create a mural. This involves cooperating, shared decision making, and completing the production of a product together.

■ Intrapersonal

When students work alone on a task in a center, they use their intrapersonal intelligence. Sometimes several students work independently, but at the same center. The following ideas suggest ways to use journals and logs to integrate independent learning and intrapersonal intelligence into the center.

Free Writing

Free writing allows students to write about anything they choose. Research shows that students have an easier time with the content and organization of a piece if they are writing about a subject that interests them.

Story Starter and Picture File

Include story starters for students to choose from in centers where journals are being used. Story starters give students ideas but allows them to choose their writing topic. Picture files also provide ideas for writing topics.

Reflection

Thinking about thinking is called metacognition. Students use this process when they answer open-ended questions such as the following:

What have I learned?

What did I like about . . . ?

What do I need to learn next?

What have I realized about . . . ?

What surprised me?

Individual reflection can be used after students have worked at solving problems or have made decisions, performed experiments or demonstrations, or composed songs.

About Projects

Projects go a step beyond centers in processing information. They move students to study content and apply what they learn in a way that brings about a deeper understanding of old and new knowledge. The students' ability to process and use information to produce a product makes the learning environment more relevant.

Projects are designed to thoroughly immerse learners in the content of study. Learners use a combination of intelligences, and choose how they will present their knowledge and their ability to use information.

Projects also provide a valuable means for transfer of learning from one area to another. They can open up a meaningful use of instruction in the classroom by extending information used in the classroom to real-world experiences. Therefore, projects often bring the world into the classroom.

Because project-based learning requires a greater depth of planning and use of information, students are called on to use both critical- and creative-thinking skills. They must also learn time management and planning skills on a more comprehensive basis. In essence, project-based learning teaches life skills that are needed to process information and create products of value to the learner and the learning environment (see fig. 4.1).

Skills Developed through Projects

Critical-Thinking Skills	Creative-Thinking Skills	Social Skills
1. Attributing 2. Comparing and contrasting 3. Classifying 4. Sequencing 5. Prioritizing 6. Drawing conclusions 7. Determining cause and effect 8. Analyzing for bias 9. Analyzing for assumptions 10. Solving analogies 11. Evaluating 12. Decision making	1. Brainstorming 2. Visualizing 3. Personifying 4. Inventing 5. Associating 6. Inferring 7. Generalizing 8. Predicting 9. Hypothesizing 10. Making analogies 11. Dealing with ambiguity and paradox 12. Problem solving	1. Respecting others 2. Working independently 3. Managing time efficiently 4. Cooperating 5. Sharing 6. Using resources effectively 7. Making choices/ decisions (From Fogarty and Bellanca, 1986)

Figure 4.1

▪ *Creating Projects*

In developing project-based learning there are two factors that need to be considered: (1) the students' ability to process information and (2) the way in which the project will be used to extend the learning experience in any particular content area. The developmental needs of the student should be considered when selecting a project assignment. The project requirements should match the learner's ability to use and process information.

In deciding how the project will be used to extend the learning experience, consider the following three questions in order to best meet the experience level of the learner as well as scheduling for instructional time.

- Will the project be an ongoing part of the instruction in one or more aspects of the content area?

- Will the project be a culminating choice to show the various aspects within a content area?

- Will the project enrich the learning environment by providing structured centers that use the content area of instruction in new ways and offer greater choices to students in the application of the instruction?

In creating projects that extend the learning experience, the following three project models further define how a project can match the teacher's goals when instructing the learner.

■ Project Models

Class Model

A class project is designed around a particular topic of study. It requires students to use information about something they have studied together as a class. For example, if a class has studied heroes, the teacher could ask each student to select a hero and create a marionette puppet using researched facts on that hero. The project could also require the student to write a script to present information about the hero and to perform a puppet play. This model is particularly suited to teaching students a more structured step-by-step process on how to plan and prepare a project.

Multiple Intelligences Model

Multiple intelligences projects are a particularly good way to bring closure to a topic of study. Although students choose their projects, which focus on different intelligences, the teacher structures the process. Multiple intelligences projects celebrate the many aspects of knowledge gained from studying a topic, an added bonus for the end of a unit of study (see fig. 4.2). Projects in this model should be structured to guide the student through the process of planning and gathering knowledge. The final construction of the project can be done outside of class.

Independent Model

Independent student projects allow students to propose and develop their own projects. After reading a student's proposal, the teacher identifies criteria for the project and provides a time line. This model allows the learner to choose the type of project and information to include. The approach works well for self-motivated learners and learners who are mature and experienced in project-based learning.

■ Working through a Project

Select a Project Model

When choosing one of the project models discussed above, consider the content to be taught as well as the ability of the learner to develop and be guided through a project. It is important to understand that project-based learning requires guidance and instruction in how to gather and organize information. Selecting a project model requires providing structure and criteria to ensure that the student can successfully put together a project that is valuable to the learning environment.

IRI/Skylight Training and Publishing, Inc.

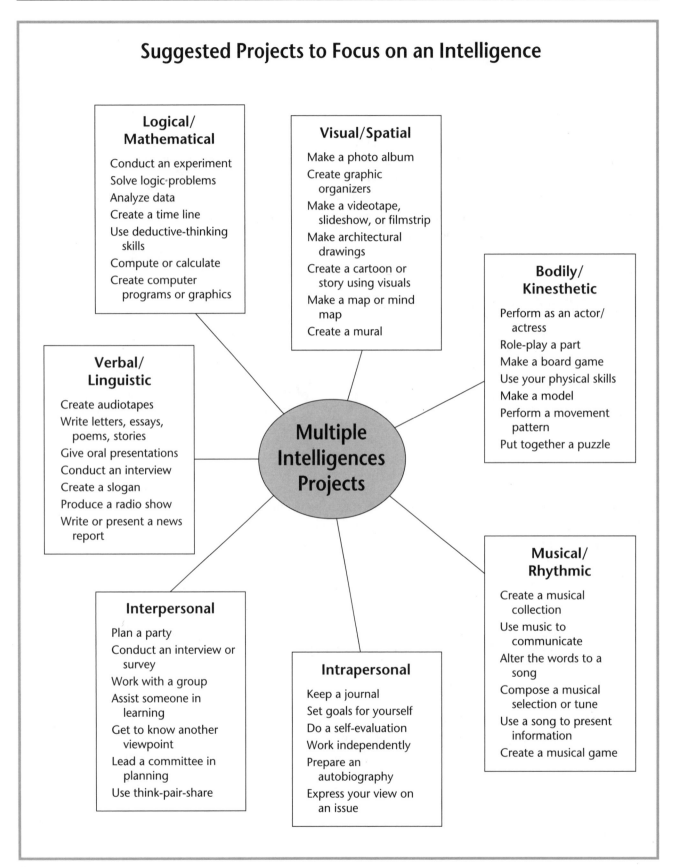

Suggested Projects to Focus on an Intelligence

Logical/ Mathematical

Conduct an experiment
Solve logic·problems
Analyze data
Create a time line
Use deductive-thinking skills
Compute or calculate
Create computer programs or graphics

Visual/Spatial

Make a photo album
Create graphic organizers
Make a videotape, slideshow, or filmstrip
Make architectural drawings
Create a cartoon or story using visuals
Make a map or mind map
Create a mural

Bodily/ Kinesthetic

Perform as an actor/ actress
Role-play a part
Make a board game
Use your physical skills
Make a model
Perform a movement pattern
Put together a puzzle

Verbal/ Linguistic

Create audiotapes
Write letters, essays, poems, stories
Give oral presentations
Conduct an interview
Create a slogan
Produce a radio show
Write or present a news report

Multiple Intelligences Projects

Musical/ Rhythmic

Create a musical collection
Use music to communicate
Alter the words to a song
Compose a musical selection or tune
Use a song to present information
Create a musical game

Interpersonal

Plan a party
Conduct an interview or survey
Work with a group
Assist someone in learning
Get to know another viewpoint
Lead a committee in planning
Use think-pair-share

Intrapersonal

Keep a journal
Set goals for yourself
Do a self-evaluation
Work independently
Prepare an autobiography
Express your view on an issue

Figure 4.2

IRI/Skylight Training and Publishing, Inc.

Choose and Plan a Specific Project

Teacher-Planned Projects

As much as possible, teachers should allow students the opportunity to explore their unique interests and ideas through projects. There will be times, however, when teachers will need to do most of the project planning. If teachers plan the projects, they should provide as much choice and variety as possible in the project assignment. If the class model is used, the selected project should target at least three of the intelligences.

After the teacher identifies the content goal, he or she will select a project focusing on one or more of the intelligences to bring about a process-learning approach. For example, a project might create a picture essay targeting the visual/spatial and verbal/linguistic intelligences. The teacher can begin the planning process using the project-planning grid (see fig. 4.3).

Student-Planned Projects

Providing structure and guidelines for students planning a project is a vital part of the learning process. Using a graphic organizer, such as the project-planning grid in figure 4.3, students can generate ideas to use either with a combination of intelligences, as in the class project model, or with specific intelligences, as in the multiple intelligences project model. Brainstorming can be done individually or in small groups. In group planning, students build on each other's ideas. These interactions provide a wider range of ideas for projects.

After evaluating each idea based on the criteria established by the teacher, students decide on a project (figs. 4.5 and 4.6). Students can then plan a rough draft of how they will put their ideas together. In most cases, the rough draft can be written down and visual organizers can be used. In some cases, however, the project will be planned entirely from drawings.

Once projects have been selected and planned, the following questions should be asked to clearly define expectations in the areas of content, presentation, and assessment:

1. What information will the completed project cover?

2. How will the project be presented to others?

3. How will the project be assessed and evaluated?

There are three ways to approach working through a project: (1) the teacher can explain and oversee the step-by-step process of completing the project within the classroom setting if the materials are available for each student; (2) the teacher can explain and oversee the decision making, planning, and fact gathering in the classroom setting, but allow students to put the project together outside of class; or (3) the students can independently plan and construct their projects outside of the classroom setting. In this case, assessment checkpoints will need to be set up with the teacher and a time line established to monitor students' progress.

Project-Planning Grid

Name _____   Level/Grade _____   Topic/Theme _____

Project-Planning Grid Using Multiple Intelligences

Verbal/Linguistic	Musical/Rhythmic	Logical/Mathematical	Visual/Spatial	Bodily/Kinesthetic	Intrapersonal	Interpersonal

Time Frame: _____

Directions: Divide a large piece of paper into several columns and write ideas for each topic on Post-it notes. Place ideas in appropriate columns for centers or projects.

Figure 4.3

IRI/Skylight Training and Publishing, Inc.

Selecting Space Projects

Verbal/Linguistic	Musical/Rhythmic	Logical/Mathematical	Visual/Spatial	Bodily/Kinesthetic	Interpersonal	Intrapersonal
• Develop a list of space vocabulary words	• Write a national anthem for one of the planets	• Graph the distances of planets from the sun or other planets	• Draw a picture of what you think a Martian looks like	• Act out man's first steps on the moon	• Interview E.T. about his trip to Earth	• Meditate on being the first person to walk on the moon
• Write a joke book for space creatures	• Write a planet rap song	• Calculate how long it would take to get to the moon traveling 100 miles per hour	• Make a model of the solar system	• Simulate the sun or the orbits of all the planets	• Role play the parts of each member of a space crew	• Describe how it would feel to be the first student in space
• Write a short story that takes place on a planet	• Create a new dance called the "Space Walk"	• Classify planets by size and temperature	• Make a clay sculpture of one of the planets	• Create a sport that would be popular in space (no gravity)	• Plan a joint space expedition with Russia	• Tell how you would feel if you did not see sunlight for a long time
• Keep a diary of a trip you took in space	• Write poetry to the music from *2001: A Space Odyssey*				• Plan a space trip with a partner	

Adapted from teachers in Cobb County, Georgia

Figure 4.4

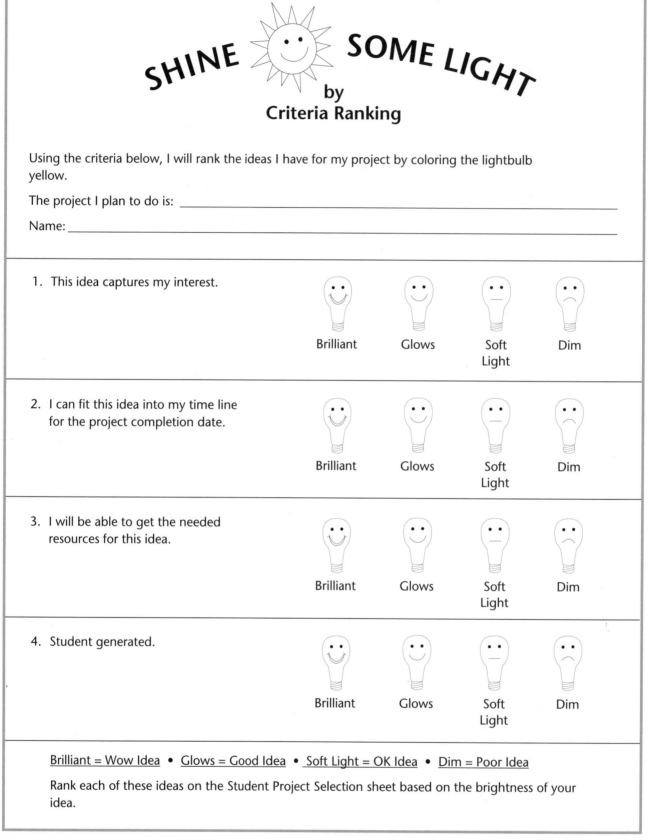

SHINE ☀ SOME LIGHT
by
Criteria Ranking

Using the criteria below, I will rank the ideas I have for my project by coloring the lightbulb yellow.

The project I plan to do is: _____

Name: _____

1. This idea captures my interest.

    Brilliant   Glows   Soft Light   Dim

2. I can fit this idea into my time line for the project completion date.

    Brilliant   Glows   Soft Light   Dim

3. I will be able to get the needed resources for this idea.

    Brilliant   Glows   Soft Light   Dim

4. Student generated.

    Brilliant   Glows   Soft Light   Dim

Brilliant = Wow Idea • Glows = Good Idea • Soft Light = OK Idea • Dim = Poor Idea

Rank each of these ideas on the Student Project Selection sheet based on the brightness of your idea.

Figure 4.5

Student Project Selection

Name: _____

The project I plan to do is: ___Hero's Hall of Fame___

Criteria

Idea List	This idea captures my interest	I can fit this idea into my timeline	I will be able to get the resources	Student generated
I will dress as a selected hero and give a speech on my life.				
Example: I will create a puppet as my hero and present my hero's life through the puppet.				
I will create a national holiday for my hero and create posters, slogans, and a documentary on my hero's contributions.				
I will write a ballad about my hero and prepare an audiotape and an ad campaign to promote my hero.				
My best idea is: _____ _____				

Figure 4.6

Assign a Project Model

After the teacher has selected the most appropriate project model, he or she must decide how to plan it using the "Eight Steps for Project Planning" (see fig 4.7). The classroom model for implementing a project guides students through the planning process to ensure successful completion. The "Eight-Step Planner" sheet (see fig. 4.8) can be used to provide an overview of the project proposal. As projects are introduced to the class, the teacher should do the following:

1. State the purpose and goals of the project.

2. Identify the concepts or ideas to be included in the project.

3. Provide a list of available sources for the students to use in gathering information.

4. Provide a choice of four to seven methods of presenting the completed project.

5. Provide a time line that includes conference dates and times to monitor the students' progress in completing the project.

6. Provide an outline to help the students organize the information needed for a rough draft.

7. Create an appropriate learning environment to celebrate the completion of the project.

8. Prepare an evaluation form for student reflection on the goals met through the planning process and completion of the project.

Provide Resources and Materials

Teachers can plan ahead and increase the interest and motivation level of students by having a wide range of reference resources available as students start their projects. The more varied the project materials, the more choices there are for students.

Leading students to other sources of information is an important part of the planning process. Students should have an understanding of the wide variety of resources available. For example, interviews, editorials, online computer networks, newspapers, businesses, and parents and other relatives can be used as resources. The kinds of resources a student uses, however, depend on the project.

Establish a Project Time Line

It is important to help students break the components of a project into scheduled completion dates so that they have time to work toward a finished product that challenges their best effort. For example, fact gathering should be followed by a rough-draft copy of information. A physical model should be preceded by a visual layout or a conceptual illustration before the actual construction of the model is begun.

Eight Steps for Project Planning

1. State the purpose and goals of your project.

2. List at least three concepts or ideas to include in your project.

3. Name at least three sources that you will use to gather information for your project.

4. Plan two or more methods you will use to present your project.

5. Schedule steps to completion on a time line to monitor your progress.

6. Prepare a rough draft plan of your project for approval.

7. Celebrate your project completion with a presentation.

8. Reflect on and evaluate the goals met.

Figure 4.7

IRI/Skylight Training and Publishing, Inc.

Eight-Step Planner

1. Project purpose and goals:	2. Project concepts to be included:	3. Sources of information:	4. How project will be presented:
5. Time line proposal:	6. Rough draft planning approval:	7. Celebration type and date:	8. Reflections:

Figure 4.8

IRI/Skylight Training and Publishing, Inc.

In establishing a time line for a project, the teacher must help the students consider the amount of time necessary for planning the project, adjusting the plan, conferencing, gathering resources and background information, constructing the project, and celebrating the completed work. Students and parents should be informed of specific dates by including them in the assignment write-up. These dates should include conferences and planning assignments required at the conferences, the final project due date, and the date for presentation and celebration of the projects.

Teachers should consider how much time students need to adequately plan and pace work. In general, a project should last no longer than six weeks. Many projects fit well into a four-week period, depending on how much time is devoted to it each day or week. Take into consideration the level of planning required and make it age-appropriate for the learner. Spending too much time planning a project can leave the student unmotivated and take away from the overall educational values gained.

The time line for any project depends on (1) the time that can be devoted to the project and (2) the nature of the project. In light of its importance, the planning process should be done within structured instructional time. Often, the project can be completed outside the school setting after planning is approved by the teacher. This allows for a wider use of materials such as personal computers and art supplies.

The time schedule established should maintain motivation, accountability, and consideration for the schedule demands of each student. Schedules should also take into account those students who require instructional modification.

The student project-planning flow chart provides an overview of the process of going through the project toward the final celebration or presentation (see fig. 4.9).

Conferences for Assessment and Guidance

Planning Conferences

Planning conferences should be included in the planning process. Conferences can be conducted within the classroom setting, with students individually, or with small groups of students who are working on similar types of projects. Students can conference with the teacher, a parent, or their peers, depending on the type of project and the wishes of the teacher. The conference provides further guidance in the planning process.

Students can outline their projects to prepare for the conference using the planner preview (see fig. 4.10), and its eight project-planning steps. A list of the required criteria for the project, given to students prior to the planning conference, should be used to monitor each student's progress in the planning process.

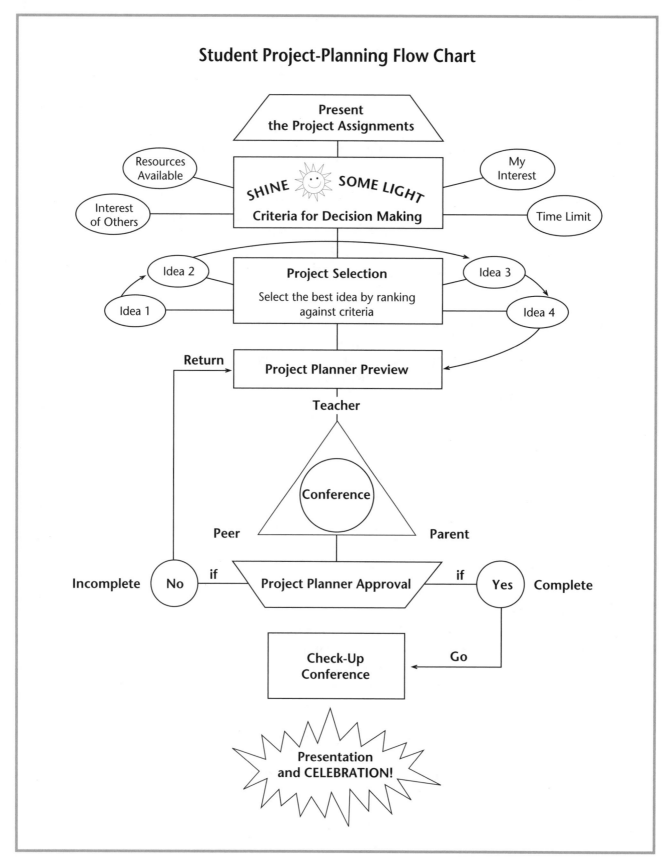

Figure 4.9

Another conference should be scheduled when the students are midway through their projects. This conference is a key component in the overall assessment of a project. It acts as a checkpoint to help correct any misconceptions and to further encourage the student before the final stages of the project. This conference also helps reinforce students' accountability.

Suggested Types of Conferences

The process of planning and working on the projects should include an ongoing assessment through the conferences. Conferences allow for evaluation and reflection. The student, teacher, parents, or peers can assess progress on the project and consider possible changes to the plan. Ongoing assessment teaches students the value of making improvements and rethinking ideas.

STUDENT/TEACHER CONFERENCE

The student/teacher conference is recommended if the use of projects is new to a class. This approach provides more direct individualized assessment of the student. It also gives immediate feedback and guidance throughout the planning process.

The student and the teacher meet on a preassigned day for a five-to-ten-minute conference to discuss and review the completed planner preview sheet prepared by the student. After this first conference, the student completes the project planner sheet (see fig. 4.11). A follow-up conference is helpful in guiding students through a time line based on the completed project planner. The project planner gives the detailed plans for the project, provides space for the teacher's comments and assessment, and an area for students to note unforeseen problems encountered in working through the project.

CONFERENCE WITH LOGS AND JOURNALS

Students can keep a daily or weekly log of their work on a project, including a planning schedule that outlines how they will break the project into segments. They can keep track of when they complete each segment and record any problems found in completing a task.

Teachers can help students assemble their logbook and explain how to keep a daily or weekly log of their work. Using the log/journal, students can conference with the teacher or their peers to discuss their progress and problems. The log/journal becomes an artifact for teachers to use in the final assessment of the project.

PEER-TO-PEER CONFERENCE

Students can use the peer checklist to conference with each other (see fig. 4.12), assess the criteria requirements for the project, and track their progress. These conferences can be managed like a buddy system in which partners are accountable to each other on a weekly basis. They can use the checklist planner to plan and complete the project. After students turn it in for the teacher's final evaluation, the teacher should give feedback prior to each conference and then conduct a culminating conference with both partners prior to the completion of the project.

Note: The Planner Preview should outline the information the student plans to include in the complete project.
For example:
- If the project is a model to be built, it should be illustrated and labeled to show the planning
- If the project is a book, each page should have a layout with the wording and pictures
- If the project is a skit, there should be a script written outlining the characters, the lines, the props needed, and a clear sequence of the events to take place

---

Planner Preview

Student Name: _____

The project I chose is: _____

Project due date: _____

A. Write a brief description of how you plan to present your idea in this project.

_____

_____

Example: I plan to dress as Amelia Earhart and tell about my life.

B. List resources you plan to use and material you will need for your project.

Resources: Ex.: Biography on Amelia Earhart _____

Ex.: Encyclopedia _____

_____

Materials: Costume—aviator's jacket _____

_____

C. Provide a graphic or visual layout describing how your project will look when completed.
(e.g., Sketch how you would look as Amelia Earhart.)

D. Provide an outline for your completed project. The outline should show the main idea included in your project.

Example: Research on Amelia Earhart
      A. Birth   B. Childhood   C. Marriage   D. Flight around the world

Things I would like to ask or I feel I need help on:

Student Question 1:

Teacher Answer:

Student Question 2:

Teacher Answer:

Figure 4.10

IRI/Skylight Training and Publishing, Inc.

Project Planner

Name: _____ Date: _____

Project title: _____

Description of project idea: _____

My calendar planner of things to do:

I plan to: _____

Week of: _____

Completed: _____

Not Completed: _____

I plan to: _____

Week of: _____

Completed: _____

Not Completed: _____

I plan to: _____

Week of: _____

Completed: _____

Not Completed: _____

I plan to: _____

Week of: _____

Completed: _____

Not Completed: _____

Problems and help needed (write as questions).

1.

Teacher comments:

2.

Teacher comments:

3.

Teacher comments:

4.

Teacher comments:

Figure 4.11

IRI/Skylight Training and Publishing, Inc.

STUDENT/PARENT LOG

Communicating with parents and involving them in the planning process can add to the quality of the project. Children can maximize the benefits of the learning experience if parents clearly understand the assignment and help their child with the planning process.

In a student/parent log, the student and parent work together on a weekly assessment of the progress made. As the student sets the project goals for the week, the parent helps assess the progress made on the goals.

The parent/student checklist (see fig. 4.13) provides teachers with a structured assessment to monitor home progress and provide feedback on improving the planning process to meet the required criteria. It is important that teachers monitor the progress being made at home and that communication is effective to assure a successful planning process between the parent and child.

■ Final Assessment

Teacher, student, peer, and parent evaluations can be used individually or in combination as a final evaluation of the completed projects.

Teacher Evaluation

Evaluate the projects based on preestablished criteria. Subjective personal comments should be given to provide positive feedback and constructive ideas that can be used in future projects. These comments should relate to the project's organization or the thinking skills used.

Teacher assessments can be categorized into four general areas: planning, the final product, presentation, and the student's evaluation and reflection. Using the criteria established in assigning the project, a teacher can assess the aspects of a project based on a point system. Each area or item listed on the assignment sheet should be assigned a point value and referred to when evaluating the final product.

Student Evaluation

After completing a project, students should evaluate whether or not their work meets the required criteria. They can reflect on their work, noting improvements they could make on their current and future projects. Reflections are an intrapersonal expression of the students' views of their project work and what they learned. They can be a valuable tool for planning projects in the future. The following questions for reflection will provide insight into the learning experience:

1. What did you learn in working on this project?

2. What would you do differently next time? What would have made it better?

Peer Checklist

Name: _____

Peer buddy: _____

Date: _____

Project title: _____

Project description: _____

My calendar planner of things to do:

A. Things I plan to do this week (buddy initials required):

1. _____   Complete_____   Incomplete ___

2. _____   Complete_____   Incomplete ___

3. _____   Complete_____   Incomplete ___

4. _____   Complete_____   Incomplete ___

Buddy checkup: Rate your buddy's progress this week:

/——————————————/——————————————/

needs help   on schedule   ahead of schedule

Problems and help needed:

1.

2.

3.

Teacher comments:

Figure 4.12

IRI/Skylight Training and Publishing, Inc.

Parent/Student Checklist

Name: _____

Date: _____

Project title: _____

Project description: _____

My calendar planner of things to do:

A. Things I plan to do this week (parent initials required):

    1. _____   Complete_____   Incomplete ___

    2. _____   Complete_____   Incomplete ___

    3. _____   Complete_____   Incomplete ___

    4. _____   Complete_____   Incomplete ___

Student reflections:

Things I feel were successful this week:

1.

2.

3.

Things I felt frustrated about this week:

Things I have questions about and need help on:

Teacher comments:

Figure 4.13

IRI/Skylight Training and Publishing, Inc.

3. List the materials/resources you would have liked to have had. List the materials/resources you used.

4. Make a step-by-step list of what you did to complete your project. How else might you use these techniques?

5. What was the most difficult part of the project?

6. What was your favorite part of the project?

7. What did you learn about your abilities as you worked on this project?

8. What kind of help did you get during this project?

9. What risks did you take?

10. What intelligence did you use most?

11. What were your successes during the project?

12. What did you learn about yourself?

13. How well did you carry out the project?

Peer Evaluation

When a peer evaluates another student's work based on the criteria outlined for the project, the peer learns how to analyze the project for different criteria. Peer evaluation requires that you identify the areas to be evaluated and include clearly defined questions to be answered. The peer evaluation can be both objective and subjective, but it must be designed to provide constructive comments for the student being evaluated. Peer evaluations can be used as information for a teacher's final evaluation.

Parent Evaluation

Just as with peer evaluations, teachers can give parents guidelines for areas to be evaluated. For example, a teacher may request that the parents evaluate whether the student has met the expectations for the project. Or, the parents may be asked to reflect on their child's progress in the planning and construction of this project or on how they think their child's thinking skills improved.

Parents have a unique perspective often not seen by a teacher. They may even be able to suggest ways to develop more successful project assignments. Parent evaluations can be considered during the final evaluation of the student's work.

Teacher Project Reflections

Every project assignment should be evaluated by the teacher in order to improve project planning. A teacher reflection sheet is one of the most valuable pieces of information in planning future projects. The sheet should include space for teachers to reflect on things in the project-planning process that should be kept, thrown out, or adapted and adjusted (see fig. 4.14).

Teachers should consider all feedback from the project conferences and planning process, including parent and student evaluations. This ongoing assessment will improve project teaching and help teachers retain information over time.

■ *Celebrating*

There are many ways to celebrate and recognize the hard work and creative expressions of individual students. Plan project celebrations in a way that creates fun and excitement in revealing the completed projects. They can range from simple celebrations to elaborate events. Here are a few suggestions:

- Build the celebration around a theme. An event, such as a picnic, party, fair, banquet, or circus, allows greater student participation.

- Create a museum to attractively display students' work, such as a wax museum of students dressed in character, or theme museums on topics such as sports, presidents, or inventions.

- Invite parents or other classes to view the projects.

- Plan special celebration days, such as Invention Convention, Celebration Day, or Earth Watch.

- Display projects in the school library or learning center.

- Organize a day for students to show projects and display their talents through plays, skits, songs, stories, or debates.

Celebrating the completion of a project is a vital part of recognizing each student's unique contribution to a project. The celebration can include any form of recognition using a shared experience.

Teacher Reflection

Unit of Study: _____

Date: _____

Things to Keep **Plus (+)**	
Things to Throw Out **Minus (–)**	
Things to Adapt and Adjust **Adjust (?)**	

Figure 4.14

IRI/Skylight Training and Publishing, Inc.

Picture-Essay Project

The following is a detailed project example for upper elementary and middle school students. This is an excellent choice as a first project to introduce students to the complex *process* of working through and completing a project. Use the classroom setting as much as possible to guide students through the steps toward completing the project as discussed in the previous chapter.

Assignment

Use pictures to create a big book that tell a story, such as a report of a recent field trip, a how-to manual, or a documentary on the subject of your choice.

Materials

- 3 sheets of white poster board cut in half to make six book pages
- 24 pictures (these can be photographs, drawings, or clips from magazines, catologs, etc.)
- a computer, paint, fabric, stick-on letters, markers (anything that could be used in creating a book)

The picture-essay book will have six pages: a cover with the title, author's name, and an introduction with a brief summary

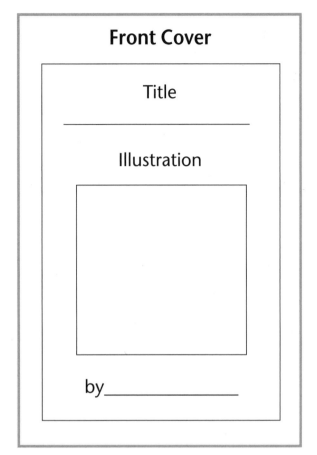

Figure 5.1

Figure 5.2

and publishing date (see figs. 5.1 and 5.2); three content pages (see fig. 5.3); and a back page with the author's biography. Work on the book can begin in class, but completion of the project will be done at home.

Requirements

Each criteria below must be included in the finished project to get full credit. Be sure that students are aware of the specific criteria and expectations before beginning work on the project. The following is a point scale that can be used to assess the final project:

> 25–24 points = Excellent
>
> 23–20 points = Very Good
>
> 19–15 points = Satisfactory
>
> 14 or below = Needs Improvement

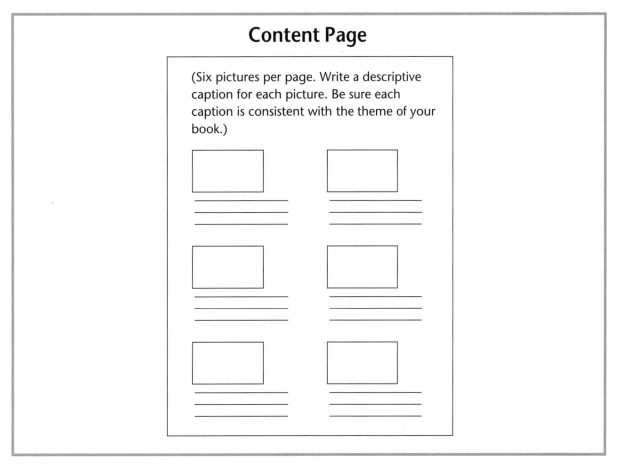

Content Page

(Six pictures per page. Write a descriptive caption for each picture. Be sure each caption is consistent with the theme of your book.)

Figure 5.3

Pictures

There must be twenty-four pictures in the book. Points will be given at the planning conference with the teacher.

> 24 pictures—5 points
>
> 23–22 pictures—4 points
>
> 21–20 pictures—3 points
>
> 19–18 pictures—2 points
>
> 17 or fewer pictures—1 point

Biography

Students should write a paragraph about who they are, including where and when they were born, their educational background, and where they have attended school. They can tell about their family, pets, and special interests. Students should write their biography as if they were writing about a person other than themselves.

Theme

The picture-essay book must use a title with a theme consistent with the category selected. The following categories can be considered:

Autobiography   Documentary

How-To   Poetry

Fairy Tale   Song

ABC

Theme carried out on all pages—5 points

Theme lacking in one area—4 points

Theme lacking in more than one area—3 points

Layout

Border on each page—1 point

Captions written under each picture—1 point

Color and design added to the pages—1 point

Neatly written, applied, or produced letters—1 point

Neatness in construction of bookbinding—1 point

Creativity

Originality, shows uniqueness in idea—1 point

Flexibility, shows ability to use theme idea in different ways—1 point

Fluency, shows ability to generate many examples; the story has a flow—1 point

Elaboration, shows ability to give detail in expressing ideas and in drawing designs—2 points

Presentation

Effective explanation of theme in the introduction—1 point

Volume and high motivation—2 points

Written evaluation of what was learned from this project—2 points

Conferencing

Teachers should let students know, in writing, when they will have a conference on their project and what they are expected to bring to the conference. A written slip can include space for a parent signature so the teacher can be sure that each student's parent(s) is aware of the project (see fig. 5.4) The project will be evaluated during the conference using a conference evaluation sheet (see fig. 5.5).

Reflection

One of the most important parts of any project is reflection. Reflection allows students to think about their work, re-create the same successes later, and avoid repeating the same mistakes again. Have the students fill out a sheet to help them think about their picture-essay project (see fig. 5.6).

IRI/Skylight Training and Publishing, Inc.

Sample Conference Slip

On _____ you will have a conference with the teacher. Come prepared to discuss your planning for this project.

Please bring your

1. Developed photos, drawings, or picture clips
2. Planning sheet for book completely filled out

I am aware of the picture-essay project. I can support the due date on this project for _____.

Parent Signature: _____

Figure 5.4

Conference Evaluation

The conference evaluaton should be assessed according to the following categories:

Pictures _____

_____

_____

Theme _____

_____

_____

Layout _____

_____

_____

Creativity _____

_____

_____

Presentation _____

_____

_____

Other comments or recommendations: _____

_____

_____

Figure 5.5

IRI/Skylight Training and Publishing, Inc.

Self-Assessment Sheet

Name:_____

Rate your project in the following areas:

1. Layout and organization.

|—————————————|—————————————|

Satisfactory   Good   Outstanding

2. Originality and creativity in theme of project.

|—————————————|—————————————|

Satisfactory   Good   Outstanding

3. Detailed informative captions.

|—————————————|—————————————|

Satisfactory   Good   Outstanding

4. Quality of pictures.

|—————————————|—————————————|

Satisfactory   Good   Outstanding

Things I've learned in this project:

Choosing pictures:

1.
2.

Planning a project:

1.
2.

Completing this project:

1.
2.

Improving my project:

1.
2.

This is how I felt about doing this project:

Figure 5.6

IRI/Skylight Training and Publishing, Inc.

SECTION TWO

Putting
It All Together

The Amazing Brain

The centers and projects presented in this chapter are designed to be used with a unit of study on the brain. Start with the anatomy of the brain. The topic of study can then branch out into a variety of related topics such as self-evaluation of one's feelings about issues, research on well-known and celebrated people in history who have made significant contributions to society, optical illusions in which the mind perceives the familiar in an unfamiliar pattern, and brain teasers that call for problem solving. For example, the Brain Power Range or the Change Your Mind projects could follow a study of self-evaluation and reflection, while one of the Writing Center activities or the Leadership Training for Heroes project could follow a study of well-known people in history.

There is an unlimited variety of possibilities that can be explored through the study of the brain. Providing choice will increase the students' opportunities to select and develop an area of interest in any one of the targeted intelligences.

■ Centers

Verbal/Linguistic

Writing Center

Materials: writing supplies

Reflect on one or several of the following topics:

1. When I am faced with a problem, these are the steps I take to solve it. (Write out your thinking process.)

2. The smartest person I know is _____ because (give several reasons).

3. A man named Dr. Howard Gardner has spent a lot of time studying the different ways one learns. A famous saying of his is, "It is not how smart you are, but how you are smart." What does this mean to me?

4. How, where, and when do I study the best? What is the worst situation for me to study in?

Reading Center

Note to teacher: Add a "stretch the mind" collection of brain teasers, riddles, jokes, story problems, and mysteries to the reading center. Consider including props in the center such as magnifying glasses, a detective cap like Sherlock Holmes', a raincoat like Columbo's, several pairs of glasses with no lenses, and bookmarks with question marks on them. Other good "brainy" additions to the reading center include encyclopedias and articles about the brain. Students can use information from these sources to draw a picture of their brains, to study and draw the brains of different animals, or to graph animals' brains according to size.

Visual/Spatial

Wire Your Brain

Materials: seven different colors of long, thin wire

Use different colors of wires to create a design of your brain. Each color can represent one of the seven intelligences. Long lengths of colored wire can represent areas of strength, medium lengths for those mediocre intelligences, and short lengths for weak areas. Students can weave and mesh the wire to show that the brain is as "unique as a finger print."

Bodily/Kinesthetic

Exercise Pulsation

Materials: stop watch

Find a partner and adopt the names "A" and "B." The A's will do an exercise first and the B's will check their partner's pulse rates. The A's will chart their pulse rates and then the partners will switch roles. The following are some examples of exercises you can do:

- run in place
- touch your toes five times
- hop on one foot
- creep along slowly like a turtle
- leap like a frog four times
- touch your toes ten times
- clap your hands eight times

Logical/Mathematical

Favorite Things

Materials: a variety of magazines

Look at a variety of pictures in magazines and think about things you like and don't like. Cut out pictures that show your likes and dislikes and fill in a chart about yourself based on the pictures you have chosen (fig. 6.1).

In the Bag

Materials: five paper bags, each labeled with one of the five senses (sight, smell, touch, taste, hearing); a variety of pictures that represent things we see, smell, touch, taste, and hear

Take turns choosing a picture. Decide which bag the picture should be placed in and why. Brainstorm the different ways you use your senses.

Musical/Rhythmic

Music for Imaginative Thinking

Materials: cassette player, a variety of music

In groups of four or five, listen to ten musical selections that have different tempos (beats), themes, and moods. As the music is played, listen to and write down your impressions on the easy-listening chart (fig. 6.2). Listen to the music again and draw pictures of what the music made you think of.

Favorite Things Chart

	Foods	Places to Be	School	Colors	Leisure Time
Likes					
Dislikes					

Figure 6.1

Music for Imaginative Thinking

Selection #	Colors	Country	People & Events	Season/Time of Year	Feelings
1					
2					
3					
4					
5					
6					
7					
8					
9					
10					

Figure 6.2

Interpersonal

Airplane Directions

Materials: paper

Create a paper airplane. Then find a partner and take turns giving each other oral directions on folding the paper to make an airplane identical to your own. When you are giving the directions, do not let your partner see the folded airplane. When the plane is completed, compare your plane to the one your partner made using your directions.

Intrapersonal

Metacognition

Materials: tape recorder

Tape record, draw, or write directions explaining how to do a task. Which intelligences did you use to give the directions? For example, give directions for getting from your home to school or for baking cupcakes. A more challenging example is to describe, step-by-step, how you solved a brain teaser.

Other Ideas for Amazing Brain Centers

Unit of focus: _____

Verbal/Linguistic:	**Musical/Rhythmic:**
Logical/Mathematical:	**Visual/Spatial:**
Bodily/Kinesthetic:	**Intrapersonal:**
Interpersonal:	**Arrangement Tips:**

Figure 6.3

IRI/Skylight Training and Publishing, Inc.

Centers for the Amazing Brain:
My Plan for Implementation

Unit of focus: _____

Targeted Intelligence: **Materials:** **Task:**	**Targeted Intelligence:** **Materials:** **Task:**
Targeted Intelligence: **Materials:** **Task:**	**Targeted Intelligence:** **Materials:** **Task:**
Targeted Intelligence: **Materials:** **Task:**	**Targeted Intelligence:** **Materials:** **Task:**
Targeted Intelligence: **Materials:** **Task:**	**Targeted Intelligence:** **Materials:** **Task:**

Figure 6.4

■ *Projects*

Verbal/Linguistic

Leadership Training for Heroes

Studying great people in history makes you aware of the traits and achievements of leaders. Through this study, you will recognize how leaders positively influence others. You can then analyze your own interactions with peers and identify how you can become a leader yourself.

Select a well-known figure in politics, science, law, sports, entertainment, or the arts whom you consider to be a hero. After researching the hero's life, become your hero and write a three-to-five-minute speech about yourself. Include information about the hero's early life, accomplishments, and disappointments. You can come to school as your hero on the day you present your speech.

Create a Venn diagram or reflection chart to show how you are similar to and different from your hero. Include at least fifteen comparisons in your chart, using pictures, words, or drawings. Be prepared to present your chart to the class.

Food for Thought

Create a restaurant menu that is suitable to feed an I.Q. Make up a clever name for the restaurant, such as "The Einstein Eatery." Menu items should include entrees, appetizers, vegetable dishes, desserts, and beverages. Each menu area should have at least two selections with creative brain-related names and a description of the main ingredients (e.g., Green Genius Salad—an intelligent combination of leafy green lettuce, raisins, and tomatoes topped with Smart Choice ranch dressing).

Advertise your restaurant in a commercial by videotaping your present menu demonstrating how to prepare one of the famous dishes enjoyed at the restaurant.

Brainy Sayings

Try to think of as many "brainy" sayings as you can. Next, create a humorous cartoon to depict each phrase. Then compile your brainy sayings and illustrations into a book. Include at least a dozen brainy sayings in your book. Idioms such as "she's a brain," "I'm losing my mind," "he's out of his mind," "what a birdbrain," or "it's all in your head" are good examples.

Visual/Spatial

Mind Connections

This project involves creating an architectural layout of your brain that shows which of your intelligences are strong and which are weak. First, draw an outline of your brain. Describe the seven intelligences and evaluate yourself by coloring your brain using different colors in different-sized sections according to your strengths in each intelligence. Next, using this architectural layout, create a head sculpture by covering with colored wire a head form made of Styrofoam, clay, or papier-mâché. The wire colors can be different for each intelligence. Strengths can be shown using a larger mass of wire in the color of the strong intelligence, and weaknesses can be shown using a smaller portion of wire in the color of the weak intelligence. The wire sculpture of your brain should be displayed next to the architectural layout as an illustration of the planning process.

Get the Big Picture

Look at a variety of pictures and practice strategic thinking by drawing conclusions about what's going on in the big picture. Then, create your own pictures that tell a story. They should be poster-board sized and colorful. Present your picture to the class, and have your classmates write a short story explaining what is happening. Everyone in class should compare ideas and conclusions about the big picture.

Bodily/Kinesthetic

Get in Touch with Your Senses

(*Note to teacher:* Collect boxes of various sizes and place a different object inside each box. Some of the objects should be completely hidden; place some so they can be partially viewed through a spy hole.)

Use only one of your senses to determine the contents of each box. Try using a sock glove to make your "sensing" of the object more difficult. Record your findings and use them to help you make an educated guess about the contents of each box (see fig. 6.5).

Sculpted Heroes

After studying and researching the life of a "great-brain hero," create a model of your hero, using accessories that reveal his or her unique characteristics and interests. Using scrap items such as wood, tin cans, and plastic bottles, build a junk sculpture. Paint and decorate your hero for display. Each great-brain sculpture should also include a title and synopsis of the life of your hero.

Logical/Mathematical

Mystery Riddle Box

Prepare for this project by listening to a short mystery that contains a riddle. After thinking about the riddle, use deductive thinking to ask the reader questions that can be answered with a "yes" or a "no" (similar to the game Twenty Questions). For example, a mystery riddle might read as follows: "John fell over dead in his cabin on the side of the mountain. His cabin was in

Get in Touch with Your Senses Chart

Box #	Number of Items	Size of Object	Texture of Object	Shape of Object	Smell of Object	Sound of Object	Type of Material
1							
2							
3							
4							

Figure 6.5

disarray with all its contents scattered everywhere. What caused his death and how did his cabin get torn up?" The questions you ask should help you solve the riddle.

(*Note to teacher:* Another way to help enhance students' deductive thinking is to provide games for students to play, such as Clue by Parker Brothers, that require them to reason and think deductively.)

Now that you have had a little practice with riddles, you are ready to create your own mystery riddle box for the class to solve. Each box should be designed with a title and look that corresponds to the mystery story. Inside the box there should be a story card and a visual clue to support the story. You will present your mystery riddle box to the class and allow the class to ask questions that can be answered with a "yes" or a "no." Offer a prize for the detective who solves your riddle.

Computer Graphic Design

Create a graphic design on graph paper. Write step-by-step directions to re-create the design on a computer using graphic-design software. Your classmates can try to re-create your design on the computer using your directions. Completed designs can be printed, compared to the original, and displayed.

Musical/Rhythmic

Name That Tune

Working with a partner, create a "Name that Tune Quiz." Choose four tunes that are familiar to the class and select portions of the songs that will not immediately reveal their identity. Then create either a slide show of images or clip pictures or create drawings that can be shown on an overhead to support the musical excerpts. Present your tunes and images to the class and challenge them to name that tune.

Brain Power Range

Perform a study to determine what time of day your mind is "fresh" and works with the greatest range of speed and accuracy. Log your results over five consecutive days. Then, observe yourself during certain periods of time using prepared problem-solving tasks to evaluate your most productive thinking. The following shows how you might log your most productive periods of time.

I work best during this time:

8:00 a.m.–11:00 a.m. [   ]

11:00 a.m.–2:00 p.m. [   ]

2:00 p.m.–5:00 p.m. [   ]

5:00 p.m.–8:00 p.m. [   ]

To complete this project, observe two other people solving problems during these same periods of time and create a chart that compares the results.

Interpersonal

Listen with Your Heart

In order to gain empathy for another person, select someone special to interview and plan a way to become involved in that person's life for one week. For example, you may choose to spend time talking with that person, write a note of encouragement, make a gift, or simply help them out. Be prepared to report to the class on who you chose, why you chose to be involved with that person, how you got involved in his or her life, and what you learned and gained from the experience.

Mind over Matter

In small groups of three or four, select a conflict situation to act out (the teacher will provide a list of conflicts, such as making a commitment to two different people for the same time and day or having to choose between the parties of two close friends). One of the groups will act out its situation for the rest of the class. After viewing the role play, the remaining students will get into their groups and act out a positive solution to the conflict. After the groups in the audience have participated in giving their solution, have the original group act out its resolution to the conflict. Continue until all project groups have had an opportunity to role-play their conflict.

Intrapersonal

How to Mind Your Own Business

Write a how-to book with fifteen ideas for "minding" one's own business. The following are some ideas:

- Ways to manage and earn money as a kid

- Ways to get your parents to say "yes"

- Ways to keep your brother or sister out of your life

- Ways to do your best in school

- Ways to plan a surprise party for someone

Bind your book and design a creative cover and illustrations for the pages.

Déjà Vu

Think about whether you have ever had the illusion that you have already experienced something that you are actually experiencing for the first time. Use one of those experiences to create a fictitious story and characters that tell about the déjà vu experience. The story should then be made into a booklet that others can read and enjoy to learn about the experience called déjà vu.

Change Your Mind

This project will explore ways to effectively break a habit by altering mind patterns using a change-your-mind journal. First, list your good and your bad habits. Then choose one habit you would like to change or stop and outline a plan to achieve that goal. For example, you might write, "I would like to stop biting my nails so they can grow out. I plan to accomplish this by wearing rubber caps on my fingers for one day and then painting them red the next day to remind me to stop. I plan to go for twenty-one days without biting my nails. My reward will be one ice-cream sundae for every seven days I am successful."

Follow these rules when creating your journal:

1. Clearly identify the habit you want to stop.

2. List the step-by-step method you plan to use to achieve the goal.

3. Conduct your plan over a twenty-one day period and chart your progress.

4. Provide rewards and incentives in your plan to encourage you to achieve your goal.

5. Keep a daily record in the change-your-mind journal that tells how you feel about your progress and how you might improve on your plan to help break the habit.

6. At the end of your twenty-one day project, write an evaluation of the successes and failures you experienced and how you plan to continue with your goal.

Discoveries of the Deep Oceans

The centers in this chapter use a sea-related theme to target specific intelligences. Although no extensive study is necessary to prepare for most of the center activities, exploring ocean life benefits students and lends depth to their learning. For example, a study of fish enriches several of the Ocean Writings center actvities as well as the Fish Kites center activity. A general study of ocean life stimulates creativity in the two Sea Murals centers.

The projects, on the other hand, do require background study—specifically relating to sharks. Students should be familiar with all aspects of sharks, including their anatomy, diversity, habitats, and the effect man has on their environment. This kind of background information will enhance all the projects in this chapter.

■ *Centers*

Verbal/Linguistic

Books on Creatures

Materials: writing and drawing supplies

Create your own creatures-of-the-deep books. Choose five to ten of your favorite creatures and then write and illustrate a story for each creature using the facts you know about them.

Sea Stories

Materials: a tape of the class's favorite sea creature story that includes a sound used as a signal to turn the page

Listen to the tape as you follow along in the book.

Sea Songs

Materials: a tape of the class's favorite song about the sea; pages containing the words to the song and plenty of room left to illustrate the lyrics

Listen to the tape and illustrate the pages that have the words to the song written on them. Then others can listen to the tape as they read the words and enjoy the illustrations.

Submarine Reading Nook

Materials: an old bed sheet (or poster board); butcher paper; table

(*Note to teacher:* You will need to help your students build their submarine.)

Create a submarine by draping a sheet or butcher paper over a table, or by using poster board to enclose it. Cut out "portholes" and doorways, climb into the "submarine," and sit on pillows while you read a wide assortment of materials related to sea life.

Boat Reading

Materials: a small boat or canoe and pillows

Enjoy the fun of being in an "ocean vessel" and reading a variety of books and other materials that are about oceans.

Ocean Writings

Materials: writing supplies

Write step-by-step directions for one of the following:

1. How to clean a fish

2. How to catch a fish

3. How to swim using the swimming stroke of your choice

4. Discover a new island on your voyage

5. How to find a buried treasure

Or, you may choose to write about one of the following:

1. Life as a fish for a day

2. A fishing adventure

3. A list of things to carry on a fishing trip

4. A list of things to carry on a discovery voyage

Visual/Spatial

Sea Murals

Materials: art supplies

Draw a sea animal or plant-life form on construction paper. When you are done with your creation, glue it onto a large sheet of blue paper hanging on a wall. As each student visits the center, he or she will draw a life form and add it to the class's sea mural.

Fish Kites

Materials: art supplies; butcher paper; old newspapers; staplers; string and/or sticks

Draw a large fish on doubled-up butcher paper. Cut out the two copies of the fish and decorate them in an imaginary or realistic way. Staple the two fish together, leaving a five- to seven-inch hole. Stuff your fish kite with balled-up pieces of newspaper and staple the hole shut. Now you are ready to display and/or fly your kite on a string or a stick.

Create a Creature

Materials: a collection of note cards, each of which lists one fact/characteristic about a sea creature

Select three to five cards and read them. Then draw a sea creature based on the characteristics/facts written on your cards. You might also want to name your creature.

Milk-Carton Boats

Materials: junk box (see appendix A); glue; scissors; milk cartons; markers; washtub or plastic pool filled with water

Cut off the top part of a small milk carton, making it a cube. Decorate the inside of the carton to look like the inside of a boat. You can add seats, flags, consoles, people, sails, etc. Launch your boat in the washtub or the pool and watch how well it floats on a voyage.

Bodily/Kinesthetic

Sink/Float Trivia

Materials: two pieces of construction paper; various objects; a dishpan or washtub filled with water

Label one sheet of paper "Sink" and the other "Float." Divide each sheet of paper into "Predicted" and "Actual" columns. Classify the objects by predicting whether they will sink or float. Record your predictions. After you have classified all the objects, place them in the water, see what happens, and record your findings. Compare what actually happened to what you predicted would happen.

Characters from the Sea

Materials: dress-up clothes; art materials; overhead projector

Role-play a character of the sea (e.g., Long John Silver) and use what you have learned about pirate life to prepare a production. You can dress like your character and use props to make a presentation to the other students who are in the center. Or, if you do not want to dress up like your character, make a puppet of your sea character, and create a skit on an overhead projector and watch it come to life.

Logical/Mathematical

Sea Puzzles

Materials: a variety of jigsaw puzzles; magazines and catalogs; cardboard; glue; scissors

Work on a jigsaw puzzle in a spot where it will not have to be moved at the end of center time. Students can come to this center at another time and work on the same puzzle.

If you wish, make your own puzzle by cutting a picture of a sea scene or creature out of a magazine, mounting it on cardboard, and cutting it into puzzle pieces. Then put the pieces back together.

Venn Play

Materials: writing supplies

Use what you know about pirate ships and modern cruise ships to explore the differences and similarities between the two. Use a Venn diagram to illustrate your comparisons (see fig. 7.1).

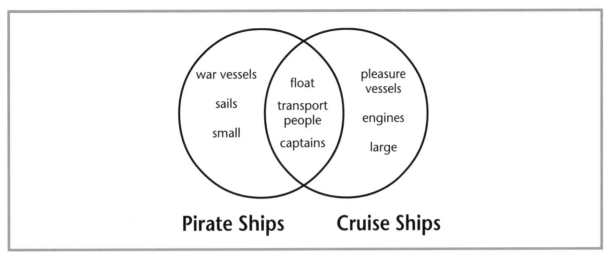

Figure 7.1

Musical/Rhythmic

Sea Sounds

Materials: some popular "beach music" tunes or sounds heard at the beach

Listen to the tape and draw or paint the images that the songs or sounds bring to your mind.

Glass Tap Rap

Materials: a variety of drinking glasses containing different amounts of water; wooden spoons

Tap the sides of the glasses with a spoon and listen to the different tones. Try to play a familiar tune. See if using an instrument other than a spoon to tap the glasses makes a different sound.

Sea Songs

Materials: writing supplies

Write a song that describes the characteristics of a sea creature and its adventures in the sea or on the shore. Use several facts you have learned about the creature in the song.

Interpersonal

More Sea Murals

Materials: art supplies

In a small cooperative group, design and create a mural of life beneath the sea. Work together to decide what the scene in the mural will be and who will create which part of the scene.

Dreaming Suitcase

Materials: paper; art supplies; cereal boxes

Brainstorm with a partner what you would need to take on a deep-sea fishing trip or a cruise to a favorite island. Decide which items can be shared and what each of you will need. Then, cut out or draw pictures of the items you have chosen and arrange them on a paper or a cereal box suitcase.

Design a Water Vehicle

Materials: drawing supplies

In a group of two to four, design a vehicle to take out to sea. First, decide what kind of adventure your vehicle is going on. Next, decide what characteristics it needs to go on your chosen adventure. Ask yourself if your vehicle has any unique qualities. Finally, draw, label, and display your vehicle.

Intrapersonal

Sea Me

Try to think of all the different sea creatures you have learned about and choose your favorite one. Use what you have learned about that creature to complete the following thought:

If I were a _____, I would . . .

Sea Storm

Brainstorm all the facts that you have learned while studying sea creatures. Pick two or three favorite facts and think about why you found them the most interesting.

Other Ideas for Discoveries of the Deep Oceans Centers

Unit of focus: _____

Verbal/Linguistic:	**Musical/Rhythmic:**
Logical/Mathematical:	**Visual/Spatial:**
Bodily/Kinesthetic:	**Intrapersonal:**
Interpersonal:	**Arrangement Tips:**

Figure 7.2

IRI/Skylight Training and Publishing, Inc.

Centers for Discoveries of the Deep Ocean:
My Plan for Implementation

Unit of focus: _____

Targeted Intelligence: **Materials:** **Task:**	**Targeted Intelligence:** **Materials:** **Task:**
Targeted Intelligence: **Materials:** **Task:**	**Targeted Intelligence:** **Materials:** **Task:**
Targeted Intelligence: **Materials:** **Task:**	**Targeted Intelligence:** **Materials:** **Task:**
Targeted Intelligence: **Materials:** **Task:**	**Targeted Intelligence:** **Materials:** **Task:**

Figure 7.3

IRI/Skylight Training and Publishing, Inc.

■ *Projects*

Verbal/Linguistic

Shark Bio

Research and write a biography on the life of a particular species of shark from birth to senior citizenship. Include a title, glossary, and facts about the author. Your book should be between fifteen and twenty pages long.

Cartoon Sharks

Create a billboard displaying shark cartoons. Consult cartoons such as "Far Side" for inspiration. Include cartoons that cover at least ten various categories of shark life, such as politics, education, family life, business, foreign affairs, or science.

Visual/Spatial

3-D Scene

Research the habitats of sharks. Create a poster-sized three-dimensional (or partly) collage of a shark scene. Give your collage a title and frame it for display.

Bodily/Kinesthetic

Sharkmobiles

Create a futuristic sharklike form of transportation that emphasizes what you have learned about shark anatomy and locomotion. Provide a diagram labeling all parts and their functions. Complete your project by constructing a model of your design.

Logical/Mathematical

Tease Your Brain

Create a shark-related brain teaser that requires logic to solve. It could be a crossword puzzle, a card game, or a game book that incorporates what you have learned about sharks. Make your product colorful and appealing.

Musical/Rhythmic

Shark Songs

Create an amusing story by producing a cassette tape that contains lyrics from a variety of popular songs. For example, you could ask the question, "Jaws, how do you feel when you're riding the waves?" and the answering song lyric could be "Like a rhinestone cowboy!"

Interpersonal

Point of View

Plan an interview that will help others understand, from your (a shark's) point of view, what sends you into a frenzy. Explain your behavior patterns and why humans often misunderstand you. Design a shark costume that you can wear during the interview. If possible, videotape the interview.

Intrapersonal

Odes to a Shark

Write a booklet of poems in which you do the following:

1. Compare yourself to a shark.

2. Appeal to the public to protect the oceans for you and the shark.

3. Explain how your life would change if you lived "in the sea."

Pirate Treasures

The following center activities and projects can be used to develop a thematic study on pirates and "treasures" found in geography, history, literature, math, and science. As a theme, the discovery of treasure appears in many aspects of learning and integrates skills from many disciplines.

Pick and choose those center activities and projects that will offer choices each student can use to explore topics associated with the treasure seekers of old. An integration of activities and projects about pirates of the 1500's and the 1600's— a subject most students find fascinating—provides opportunities for students to develop a variety of skills. These skills can include: summarizing, organizing, mapping, and analyzing. The topic, pirate adventures, encourages creative thinking through such activities as designing maps and creating stories.

■ Centers

Verbal/Linguistic

Pirate Treasures

Materials: writing supplies

Research the life of a pirate of your choice. Then, imagine you are a pirate and write a story about yourself incorporating what you have learned in your research.

International Mystery Treasure Hunt

Materials: writing supplies

Pretend that you are taking another person to an island for a mystery treasure hunt. Use what you know about voyages and treasure hunts to write a step-by-step voyage travel agenda.

Treasure Troves

Materials: treasure-related reading materials and pictures

Use resources, such as articles, pictures, and other research materials, to explore and read about treasure digs, treasure dives, mine explorations, caves, and pirate voyages and adventures. Write summaries of the information you have discovered. These summaries can be added to the class's treasure reference guide, and referred to during other activities.

Visual/Spatial

Ship Ahoy Flag

Materials: straws; construction paper; sticks; crayons; other art supplies

After you have researched the various flags flown on historic pirate ships, design and construct a pirate flag of your choice that symbolizes either a specific pirate or you.

The Hidden Picture

Materials: art supplies

Create a picture that contains a hidden design or element, such as coins or jewels hidden in an outdoor scene, or pirate-related objects, such as anchors or flags. Use color and shape to "hide" your pirate-related objects.

Bodily/Kinesthetic

Walk the Plank

Materials: writing supplies; blank notecards; masking tape

Working in pairs, create fact cards that reflect what you have learned about pirates in this unit of study. Write questions on one side of the card and the answers on the other side.

Divide a "plank" into eight to ten spaces using masking tape on the floor. While one player stands at the beginning of the plank, the other reads a question. If the person on the plank answers the question incorrectly, he or she must move forward one space. If he or she answers correctly, the next question is asked. The game proceeds until twelve questions have been asked or the person walking the plank falls off, whichever comes first. Record where your partner ended up and then reverse roles.

Knot Center

Materials: jute, yarn, or rope; an assortment of cards providing step-by-step instructions and illustrations on tying a variety of knots

Using the cards found in the center as a guide, attempt to tie a variety of knots. Explore whether it is more difficult to tie the knots using thin yarn or thick rope. While you are tying your knots, think about what pirates might have used them for and imagine how you could use them.

Logical/Mathematical

Compass Orienting

Materials: compass; pencils, crayons, or markers; paper

Use a compass to determine the direction of the classroom. Draw the classroom, and then label your drawing with N, W, etc. Include major "landmarks" of the classroom in your drawing and see if you can find four distinct objects that are located at the cardinal direction points, such as the clock is due north.

Create Treasure Maps

Materials: drawing supplies

Draw a map of a place you consider a "treasure" and/or of a new place to visit. Include labeled landmarks and a compass rose to indicate your understanding of maps.

Musical/Rhythmic

Drum Beats

Materials: island sticks; bamboo; coconuts; gourds; clay (mud); beans; shells; jute (vines); oatmeal boxes; paper-towel holders; cans; straws

Make an island instrument from common materials found around your house and any available natural island materials. Think about what kind of sound you would like it to make and what it could be used for. After you have made your instrument, name it.

Interpersonal

Treasures by the Dozen

Work in pairs to do the following:

1. One person names and performs three actions.

2. The other person repeats these actions in the same sequence and then adds another.

3. Now the first person repeats the other person's four actions and adds one.

The game continues until twelve actions have been created.

Maps to the Treasure

Materials: writing and drawing supplies

Working together in pairs, think of ways to find a hidden treasure in an imaginary place of your choice. Once you have agreed on a treasure and the place it is hidden, draw a map and write step-by-step directions that lead to your treasure.

Intrapersonal

Treasure Bag

Materials: art supplies; magazines

Think about those things or ideas that represent who you are and what you treasure most. Decorate a bag to represent your treasures. Then draw or cut out of magazines pictures of three to five of your favorite objects and place them inside your bag.

Buried Treasure

Materials: Pringles cans or shoe boxes

Think about the things you treasure in life and what they say about you as a person. Choose one or two objects that represent you and place them inside the Pringles can or shoe box. Once everyone in class has completed this activity, bury your treasures outside for someone to discover in the future, or share them with another class at your school or another school.

Bottle Your Life

Materials: empty two-liter bottles

Write an autobiography of your life that discusses modern conveniences, pop culture, your family, day-to-day life, and anything else that would explain to someone what life is like today. Sign and date your document. After everyone in class has completed this activity, bury the containers as a group or exchange them with another class.

My World in a Box

Materials: cardboard boxes; art supplies

Decorate a cardboard box on both the inside and the outside with drawings illustrating the world in which we live. You can draw your family, friends, inner thoughts, favorite possessions, books, clothes, movies, hobbies, foods, and role models.

IRI/Skylight Training and Publishing, Inc.

Other Ideas for Pirate Treasures Centers

Unit of focus: _____

Verbal/Linguistic:	Musical/Rhythmic:
Logical/Mathematical:	Visual/Spatial:
Bodily/Kinesthetic:	Intrapersonal:
Interpersonal:	Arrangement Tips:

Figure 8.1

IRI/Skylight Training and Publishing, Inc.

Centers for Pirate Treasures:
My Plan for Implementation

Unit of focus: _____

Targeted Intelligence: **Materials:** **Task:**	**Targeted Intelligence:** **Materials:** **Task:**
Targeted Intelligence: **Materials:** **Task:**	**Targeted Intelligence:** **Materials:** **Task:**
Targeted Intelligence: **Materials:** **Task:**	**Targeted Intelligence:** **Materials:** **Task:**
Targeted Intelligence: **Materials:** **Task:**	**Targeted Intelligence:** **Materials:** **Task:**

Figure 8.2

IRI/Skylight Training and Publishing, Inc.

▪ *Projects*

Verbal/Linguistic

Journaling

Watch a pirate video such as "Treasure Island." Pretend that you are Long John Silver and write a journal of your thoughts, findings, and reactions to the adventures you experienced in the movie. You might even want to come up with a different ending to your adventure and log your reactions to it.

Pirate Facts

Write a book that will clear up the difference between facts and fiction about pirates. Include answers to the following eight questions:

1. Why did pirates put a skull and crossbones on their flags?

2. Did pirates actually force people to "walk the plank"?

3. Was there a real Long John Silver?

4. Was Blackbeard a real man?

5. Was there really a Captain Hook?

6. Did places such as the Spanish Main or the Barbary Coast actually exist?

7. (Make up your own)

8. (Make up your own)

If You Knew What I Know

Write a comic book that is entitled "Things Only a Pirate Should Do" by Crooked High Seas. The book should be eight to ten pages long and include instructions and illustrations on how to make the most of your pirating skills. If you want, make your comic book humorous.

Visual/Spatial

Pirate Pictures

Research and report on an artist who is well known for his or her artwork with pirates as their subjects (e.g., Howard Pyle). Include in your report where the artist was from, when he or she lived, and a list of his or her paintings. Using the information that you have gathered, create your own picture of some aspect of pirate life.

IRI/Skylight Training and Publishing, Inc.

Cave Exploration

Create a cave diorama that demonstrates what you know about caves; include at least five cave formations. Make a mini-reference book that illustrates and defines your formations.

Bodily/Kinesthetic

Read My Code

Research the signal codes ships use to communicate. Make up your own signal code flags of the alphabet. Once you have taught the others in your class your flag code, present three coded messages, such as a plea for help, that a ship might send to another ship.

Pirate Play

Working in a small cooperative group, write a script and assign characters to role-play a conflict between pirates in a mutiny on the high seas, a treasure discovery, or a pirate attack. As you are writing the script, think about how you would react to the situation if you were a pirate. Role-play before the entire class.

Logical/Mathematical

Treasure Map

Create a treasure map that maps the route from your school to _____(fill in with an imaginary or a real place), where you have hidden a treasure. Include the following map features:

1. Poster board sized and stained to show the aging process.

2. Drawings outlined in black ink, with color added.

3. Five dangerous-to-maneuver obstacles between school and _____. These obstacles should be labeled.

4. A key that interprets symbols, mileage, and directions. Include a biographical sketch of you, as the pirate, and the content of your treasure.

Hide and Seek

Plan a worldwide treasure hunt by selecting a place to hide an imaginary treasure. Present eight riddles as clues that will lead the treasure seekers to the treasure by means of research and a world map.

The Name of the Game

Research facts about treasure ships and treasures recovered from sunken vessels. Create a board game about buried treasures from three famous treasure ships that you have learned about during your research. Make up the game's name, the rules of the game, and game pieces, such as coins and/or famous pirates.

Musical/Rhythmic

A Song in My Heart

Using a tune such as "The Farmer in the Dell," create a pirate songbook that contains at least seven stanzas about the life of a sea pirate you have researched. Your songbook should have a title, a stanza on a separate, illustrated page, and a dedication. Create a sing-along tape to accompany your songbook.

Island Instruments

Imagine you are a pirate stranded on an island. You decide to spend some time inventing an instrument made out of materials found on the island. Design, make, and name your instrument. When you are done, write a how-to manual so that others can build your instrument.

Interpersonal

Pirate Party

In a group of three to five students, plan a "Buccaneer Beach Party" for the entire class. Include a menu of foods, each with a creative pirate name. Plan and design party decorations and make a souvenir for each pirate guest. Prepare five pirate games for everyone to play.

Show Time

With a partner, choose a famous pirate from among the many you have learned about. Write a script for a puppet show that will highlight the life of your pirate. Make the puppets, decide who will play which roles, and present your puppet show.

Intrapersonal

My Top Twenty

Make a list of the twenty things that you treasure the most. Create a treasure book with each treasure illustrated on a separate page in rank order, from the thing you most value to the thing you least value. Explain why you chose each of these items.

The Root of Evil

Research and study two notorious pirates. Decide what you think determines villainous and evil behavior. Make a chart that compares how villainous and evil both of these pirates were. Include on your chart five ways the pirates differed (e.g., their deeds, reputation, behavior, etc.). Finally, explain from their point of view why they chose to be a pirate.

Space Travel

The following centers and projects are designed to work with the targeted multiple intelligences in an integrated unit of study on the history and principles of aviation and space. Many of the centers and projects require background knowledge, such as the characteristics of planets for the Planet Visits center and the Planetary Travel Brochure project, and the principles of flight for the Up, Up, and Away project. Prior to introducing many of these activities, students will need instruction and resources that cover the many aspects of aviation and space exploration. For example, after Bernoulli's principle has been taught, the Bernoulli's Principle center can be opened to reinforce and develop a deeper understanding of the concept through application.

Many of the centers can be used by students of various ages by modifying the complexity of the activity. In the Aerodynamic Center, for example, younger students might create an imaginary rocket using junk box materials, while older students can create a more realistic model using a scale drawing.

■ Centers

Verbal/Linguistic Centers

Rocket Reading

Materials: five 2" x 2" boards; a small cardboard box; rope; (or just use large appliance boxes); space-related reading materials

(*Note to teacher:* In order to provide a reading environment linked to the space unit of study, create a rocket ship for students to read in. To build the ship, assemble the five 2" x 2"s into a teepee shape and tie the top with rope. Place a small cardboard box at the top to square it off. Cover the rocket with butcher paper, cut out holes for an entrance, and let the students decorate the rocket. Supply it with pillows. The ship can also be made out of several large appliance boxes that the students decorate.)

Enjoy reading a variety of space-related books as you pretend you're on the way to your favorite planet.

Create a Big Book

Materials: writing and art supplies

Using what you have learned about the planets, create a class big book. Compose a page of the book while at the center. Begin with the sentence, "If I lived on [one of the planets], I would . . . ." Illustrate your page. After each student has completed this center activity, a class book can be compiled for all to read.

Planet Visits

Materials: art supplies

Based on what you have learned, decide which planet is your favorite and why. Then, create an advertisement or a billboard that a travel bureau could use to entice visitors to your favorite planet.

Martian Talk

Materials: writing and art supplies

Begin your own Martian dictionary by coining a Martian word. On a small piece of paper, write down the word and its meaning and illustrate it. Come up with other words and follow the same procedure. When you are done, put your words in alphabetical order and assemble the pages into a dictionary. Finally, pick one or two of your favorite words and copy the pages you created for these words. Your favorite words will then be combined with the words other students have chosen into a class book of ABC space jabberwocky.

Visual/Spatial

Planet Mobiles

Materials: Styrofoam balls of all sizes; papier-mâché (see appendix B for recipe); clay; dowel rods or coat hangers; string

Create a mobile of our solar system, keeping in mind the distances between the planets and their size relative to one another.

Space Creatures

Materials: soap boxes; clay; fruit; papier-mâché (see appendix B for recipe); other miscellaneous art materials

Use your imagination to create a space creature that is either from one of the planets in our solar system or from an entirely different solar system. As you are imagining your creature, think about the possibility that where it lives might influence what it looks like.

Martian Hats

Materials: junk box (see appendix A)

Create a Martian hat using materials from the junk box. Decorate the hat with pictures, designs, and/or things that you think a Martian might do and/or like.

Etching Space

Materials: art supplies; thick black or blue tempera paint; a variety of tools for etching in the tempera

Draw a colorful puzzle design using crayons. Cover your design with a layer of fairly thick black or blue tempera paint. Use blunt scissors, a toothpick, a paper clip, or a similar object to scrape a space scene into the picture.

Space Paint Resist

Materials: art supplies; blue tempera paint

Draw and/or color a realistic or an imaginative picture of a space adventure. When your picture is done, paint over it with a thin layer of blue tempera. This will create the illusion of your space adventure showing through the blue sky.

Aerodynamic Center

Materials: junk box (see appendix A)

Use your imagination and what you have learned about space vehicles to design rockets, airplanes, helicopters, jets, or other flying objects of the future. Use materials from the junk box to build your vehicle.

Bodily/Kinesthetic

Bernoulli's Principle

Materials: 3 x 20 cm crepe or tissue paper

Get two lengths of the crepe or tissue paper and hold them in front of your mouth. In order to demonstrate air-current flow, blow over the top of the pieces of paper. Vary the rate at which you blow and see what effect it has on the paper's movement. Finally, write down or explain to someone what happened.

Flashlight Sun

Materials: globe; flashlight; class log

Working in pairs, hold a flashlight as steady as you can a few feet away from a globe while your partner turns the globe. Imagine that the flashlight is the sun and write your observations in the class log. You may also want to observe the effect of moving the flashlight closer to and further away from the globe.

Space Actions

Materials: art supplies; blank transparencies; overhead projector

Create a setting of outer space or the surface of a planet on a blank transparency. Write a script about something that happens in the setting you have created. Make puppets that will represent the character(s) in your play. Finally, turn on the overhead projector and act out your play.

Logical/Mathematical

Model of Planets

Materials: graph paper; model of the planets; ruler/tape measure; compass/protractor; colored pencils

Measure the distances between the planets and between certain planets and the sun and plot your measurements on graph paper. Make sure that you also note the size of each of the planets.

How-to Training Manual

Materials: writing supplies

Create a training manual that would teach a Martian how to do one or more of the following:

1. Blow up a balloon

2. Make a bed

3. Brush its teeth

IRI/Skylight Training and Publishing, Inc.

4. Take care of a pet

5. Fold an airplane

6. Make a peanut butter and jelly sandwich

As you are writing your directions and/or instructions, pretend that the Martian knows absolutely nothing about any of these activities.

Space Math

Materials: a variety of number-fact and word-problem cards; counters; overhead projector

Choose several of the number-fact and word-problem cards and use space counters on the overhead projector to solve the problems you have chosen.

Musical/Rhythmic

The Martian Groove

Materials: art supplies; a variety of music selections; tape recorder

Working in a small group, choose and record music that you think might be appropriate for a Martian dance. As you listen to the music you have selected, either invent and perform a Martian dance, draw a picture of Martians dancing to the beat, or create Martian puppets and have them dance to the beat.

Sounds in the "Spacey" World

Materials: tape recorder; blank tape; a variety of noisy objects

Think about what noises you might hear in space, such as airplanes, thunderstorms, etc. Use various objects to make the noises you create. Tape record your noises and then rewind your tape and listen to it. Continue to add to your space noise tape. It will become part of a class tape of space sounds that can be used during other activities.

Interpersonal

Air-Bag Flight

Materials: trash bags; duct tape; pencils; plastic straws

Working in a team of five to six students, seal the open end of a trash bag with duct tape so that no air can leak out. Place the bag flat on the floor. Each teammate will use a pencil to poke a hole into the bag. Put a plastic straw in the hole. Secure the straw with duct tape to prevent air leaks. While one of the group members sits on top of the trash bag, the others will blow into their straws as hard as they can. See what happens if everyone does not blow into their straw at the same time or if the student sitting on the bag is not sitting exactly in the center.

Future in Space

Materials: drawing supplies

Working with a partner, design an effective spaceship or space station of the future using what you have learned about outer space and space travel.

Intrapersonal

Egghead Drop

Materials: uncooked eggs; a variety of materials to cushion and protect the eggs, such as foam padding, boxes, etc.

Draw the face of an astronaut on an uncooked egg. Design and create a protective capsule for your egghead that will prevent it from breaking when dropped from a considerable height. After everyone has completed this part of the activity at the center, take the capsules on a "test flight" by dropping them from a high place such as a tree, a roof, or the top of a tall slide. See whose eggheads survived and try to figure out why.

Stamp It

Materials: a variety of art supplies

Design and draw a postage stamp that honors a space voyage, mission, or astronaut that particularly attracted your attention during this unit of study. Add your stamp to a class stamp-collection book.

Space Travel Momentoes

Materials: writing supplies

List at least ten things that you would miss if you took a two-year space voyage. Rank the items from those you would miss the most to those you would miss the least.

Other Ideas for Space Travel Centers

Unit of focus: _____

Verbal/Linguistic:	Musical/Rhythmic:
Logical/Mathematical:	Visual/Spatial:
Bodily/Kinesthetic:	Intrapersonal:
Interpersonal:	Arrangement Tips:

Figure 9.1

IRI/Skylight Training and Publishing, Inc.

Centers for Space Travel:
My Plan for Implementation

Unit of focus: _____

Targeted Intelligence: **Materials:** **Task:**	**Targeted Intelligence:** **Materials:** **Task:**
Targeted Intelligence: **Materials:** **Task:**	**Targeted Intelligence:** **Materials:** **Task:**
Targeted Intelligence: **Materials:** **Task:**	**Targeted Intelligence:** **Materials:** **Task:**
Targeted Intelligence: **Materials:** **Task:**	**Targeted Intelligence:** **Materials:** **Task:**

Figure 9.2

■ *Projects*

Verbal/Linguistic

Where in Space Is Carmen Starlego?

Carmen Starlego, an alien intergalactic "Mind Buster," has just landed on Earth. She has been known to travel through space from planet to planet seeking to destroy the memories of those on Earth. Everyone Carmen encounters is becoming an alienated alien and cannot remember who they are or where they live. Carmen's mission is to make "space cadets" of each human she meets.

Write a short story about Carmen Starlego that will knock the boosters off of Steven Spilloff and make him come after you for the movie rights to this sensational adventure story. Explain how Carmen Starlego has stolen her victims' memories and invent clues that will lead to her arrest. She will travel from planet to planet, hiding until you devise a clever way to capture this terrible intergalactic criminal known as "Mind Buster."

Astronuts

Consult a joke and riddle book, such as *Astronuts: Space Jokes and Riddles* compiled by Charles Keller, in order to inspire you to create three to five of your own space-related riddles or jokes.

For example:

> What did the space scientist find in his frying pan?
>
> Answer: An unidentified frying object.
>
> What kind of food do astronauts eat?
>
> Answer: Launch meat.

Once everyone in the class has completed their riddles and jokes, combine them and create a class book and decide on an appropriate title and illustration(s) for it.

Planetary Travel Brochure

Research a planet of your choice and create a travel brochure that provides useful travel tips for visiting that planet. The brochure should include the following information:

1. Travel time and agency
2. Mode of travel
3. How to dress for the climate
4. Dining guide
5. Currency exchange
6. Sights worth seeing

Visual/Spatial

Space Odyssey Fashion Gala

Research a planet of your choice and plan a vacation to spend there. Using your most creative and out-of-this-world fashion-designing talents, use only things you have found around your house to put together a fashionable outfit for your vacation. Encourage students to create an outfit that adapts to at least five actual physical features of the planet you have chosen to visit.

Write a short review describing the fashion features of your outfit and use it to introduce your outfit to your class as you model it at a "Space Odyssey Fashion Gala". Take turns acting as the emcee so that each of you can walk the fashion runway and model your spacey fashions.

Time Flies When You're Having Fun

Create a picture book that illustrates twelve occasions you enjoyed so much that you lost all track of time. Write each occurrence down at the bottom of a single page and illustrate it to complete your picture book.

Bodily/Kinesthetic

Up, Up, and Away

Research and experiment with various kite designs. When you have come up with a design you like, make a sketch of it and create a list of materials needed to construct your kite. You are attempting to design a kite that will meet two criteria you have selected for excellent kite quality control.

Construct your kite following the criteria necessary to meet your high standards of quality kite products. Give your kite a name and test out the standards you set for your product. Prepare a kite-shaped pamphlet that advertises your kite and points out its best features. Show off your kite on a windy "Go Fly a Kite" celebration day.

Intergalactic Interview

The Galactic Communication Network will present a flight hero from the past. Start by researching a historical aviation figure that you will impersonate in a live interview. To prepare for interview questions your classmates might ask about "you," familiarize yourself with the following information: the aviator's early life, his or her accomplishments and failures, and notable remarks he or she made. If you can, videotape your interview.

Logical/Mathematical

Inventors Space Museum

Many new discoveries are the result of space-age exploration. Research how inventions related to space exploration have produced new products such as freeze-dried foods. Come up with your own space-age invention by following the inventor's steps to discovery that you have learned about.

Start with a characteristic unique to space exploration, such as the weightlessness caused by lack of gravity. Think of activities that might be problematic in a gravity-free environment, such as brushing your teeth, making your bed, or getting dressed. Once you have identified a problem you wish to solve, brainstorm possible solutions. Set criteria to select the best solution, and put the solution you chose to the test by creating both a conceptual model, consisting of a drawing or an illustration, and a physical model, which does not need to be a working model. Present both of your models to the entire class and ask students for their reactions to and opinions of them.

Weather Watch

Graph the weather where you live on planet Earth for one month. Before you begin, predict the number of sunny, cloudy, rainy, foggy, snowy, and windy days you think will occur during the month. Record the actual daily weather on a chart at the same time every day. Compare your predictions to the actual results at the end of your research month. You may also want to compare the predictions of a resource such as the Farmer's Almanac with your actual findings. Discuss your findings in a report that includes your predictions and your data-gathering chart.

Musical/Rhythmic

Top Tunes in Space

Choose a familiar tune and create new lyrics for it that reflect a space voyage you are planning to take. Create rubber-glove puppets that will sing along with your song. Pack a travel bag filled with items that you can pull out as you and your puppets present your song. Try to include the planets you will be visiting in your lyrics. Example song:

> (To the tune of "Leaving on a Jet Plane")
>
> I packed my bags on Venus to stay
>
> I won't be back for many a day
>
> Oh, Mom, I know you'll miss me so
>
> (Pull a picture of your mom out of your travel bag)
>
> I'm leaving on a space trip
>
> Don't know when I'll be back again
>
> Please send an e-mail message to me.

Musical Video

Working with a partner, select a song you might enjoy listening to repeatedly on a space flight. For example, the astronauts on Discovery played the song "I Heard It through the Grapevine." Team up with a friend and create a music video of the song you selected that will be played on your closed-circuit space voyage. Be prepared to present your video to the class.

Space Music On the Move

Collect and tape at least four to six space and flight songs that have been used in space-related movies. Think about why these songs were appropriate for the movie and a particular scene or scenes. Tape only one to two minutes of each of your selections. On the tape, include the name of each selection, the artist, and the movie it was used in and be prepared to play your tape for the class.

Or, choose four to six songs that you think would be appropriate as background music for a space movie. The movie can be either one you have seen or a movie that you envision. Record one to two minutes of each selection. After each selection, name the piece, the artist, why you chose the music, and how it would fit into the particular scene of the movie you chose.

Interpersonal

Back to the Future

It is your mission to go back in time and find an individual who has made a contribution to the "lift-off" of the space age. Working in a small group as a TV crew member, prepare a list of questions you would like to ask a famous pioneering aviator or space explorer. Do an on-the-spot interview, complete with costumes, video camera, and news reporter. You will be broadcasting from space network GNN (Galactic Network News), the news station of the future. Don't forget to create a futuristic costume for your galactic reporter. As a group, prepare appropriate questions to present to your explorer. The answers will help future generations appreciate the history of the space age.

Solar Research Committee

With a small group, select one of the planets in our solar system (other than the Earth) to research. You may also choose the sun.

Write a report using research on the subject you selected. The report may include the planet's size, location in the galaxy, atmosphere, land formations, revolutions, possibility of life forms, discovery (when and by whom), legends and myths, etc.

Each group will create a skit based on a ten-year mission to explore alternative sources of energy found on the planet they chose. In the skit, you have set up a research space station and have collected information and discoveries that allow you to provide a full evaluation of life and energy sources on that planet. Make your skit a mixture of fact and fiction. For example, the poisonous gas rings of Saturn have made it impossible to live on the planet's surface. The "Saturnilians" have built homes that hover over the planet and can convert the poisonous gases into energy to power their capsule-like homes.

Some alternative energy-finding missions may not be successful. The skit should explain any obstacles and whether the mission was aborted and why.

Intrapersonal

Cloud Coverage

Create a cloud diary. Draw a picture for the front cover that looks like a cloud. Find some time alone to relax and study the clouds on a clear, pretty day. Use your diary to draw and label any cloud shapes you see.

While clouds can give us messages about the weather and tell us what is happening in the atmosphere, our feelings can give us messages about our personal atmosphere. Enter in your diary, on separate pages, your thoughts on the following cloud messages about the weather conditions in your life:

1. Write down the storm clouds of your life—things that upset you or make you angry.

2. Record the puffy, bright, white, sunny clouds—things that you are proud of.

3. Express your thoughts on the hazy, gray stratus clouds that warn of problems, struggles, or fears you have.

4. When clouds become too dense and full, it rains. Tell about a situation in your life that brought you to the point of tears.

5. Think about one of your best contributions and write a page or two using the following idea to get you started: "If I could move a cloud, I could help humankind by . . . ."

Flight Scrapbook

Research the history of flight and create a ten- to twelve-page scrapbook of newspaper articles, pictures, and letters written about the history of aviation. Include everything from the hot-air balloon, dirigibles, and gliders, to motor-powered planes, jet propulsion, and space rockets. At the end of the scrapbook, write a summary of the changes that have occurred in the history of flight and predict the changes you think will occur in the next twenty years.

Safety First

Invent a safety feature that will protect against collisions due to any flaw in a vehicle such as a bicycle, a tractor, roller blades, or a go-cart. Make a model of your invention, label all its parts and display it with a poster illustrating how it works.

Colors of Our World

This chapter's approach to centers and projects lends itself to targeting the visual/spatial intelligence; however, all of the intelligences are represented. The activities in this unit open up a variety of ways to view the world through color, examples of which include the Rhythms of Color and the Color of Your Week centers, as well as the Am I Blue? and the Green with Envy projects.

The following centers and projects do not require the students to have background knowledge of any specific content area. Students explore the psychology of color and the science of mixing colors in these centers and projects while investigating the components of color in the light spectrum, and through art and decorating, advertising and design, and the communication of ideas.

■ Centers

(See appendix B for a variety of recipes, many of which can be used for activities in this as well as other chapters.)

Verbal/Linguistic

Alliterations

Materials: writing supplies

Write as many alliterations as you can think of that involve color. Try to make them as long as you can and, if you want, make them funny. Here are some examples: green, grimy grease; romping, running, rosy-red roosters; and pretty, pouncing, purple, polka-dotted pandas. You might want to create a class book of your alliterations.

Color Moods

Materials: a variety of illustrated books that show a particular use of color in the illustrations (e.g., *The Napping House* by Audrey and Don Wood)

Explore the use of color by looking at and reading a variety of books with illustrations. See how the artist(s) used color to match the mood or the feelings in the story. Was blue used to show sadness? Were bright colors used in happy stories? Choose a favorite story and write about how you might use color differently in the illustrations.

Colors in Our Room

Materials: drawing supplies

Pick a color and write the name of it in big block letters on a large piece of paper. Then look around the classroom. Try to find as many things as you can that are the same color as you have chosen. Write those items around your word. After you have surrounded your color word with the names of items that are the same color, try the same thing with another color.

Visual/Spatial

Food-Coloring Dabbles

Materials: eye droppers; baby food jars; a variety of liquid food coloring

Add water to a number of baby food jars. Select a food color and use the eye dropper to add it to the jar. Repeat this with another jar, but this time, add a little more food coloring and observe how much the colored water changes in intensity. Repeat this several times and then arrange the jars from darkest to lightest in color.

Noodle Dye

Materials: one box (10 oz.) of different shapes and sizes of dried (or uncooked) pasta; gallon-sized Ziploc freezer bags; isopropyl rubbing alcohol; food coloring; wax paper

To dye pasta, add the box of noodles, two tablespoons of food coloring, and two tablespoons of alcohol to a gallon-sized Ziploc freezer bag. (*Note to teacher:* You may want to help the students with this.) Seal the bag and shake it until the noodles have absorbed all the liquid and are dyed. Spread the pasta out on wax paper to dry. Try this with a variety of different colors and observe which color the pasta absorbs best.

Use your colored pasta shapes to make a collage or a three-dimensional sculpture. (Students can use the colored pasta shapes for counters or for pattern necklaces, in their logical/mathematical activities .)

Sand Art

Materials: white sand; food coloring; isopropyl rubbing alcohol; gallon-sized Ziploc freezer bags; small glass bottles

Place the sand in a freezer bag and add two tablespoons of food coloring and two tablespoons of alcohol. (*Note to teacher:* You may want to help the students with this.) Seal the bag and shake it until all the liquid is absorbed and all the sand is dyed. Use a different freezer bag for each color. You may even wish to experiment with making colors by using one tablespoon each of two different colors. Once you have finished dyeing the sand, create sand art by arranging different colors of the sand in layers in small glass jars. Shaking the jars will disturb the colored layers. You may want to do this on purpose to see what color results from mixing all the colors you have layered together.

Projected Colors

Materials: food coloring; eye droppers; clear plastic cups; overhead projector

Turn on the overhead projector in a corner of the room. Add water to the plastic cups and place them on the projector. Add a variety of drops of food coloring to the water and observe the colors reflected on the wall. For example, mix red and yellow to make orange, and blue and yellow to make green. Try making shades of colors such as adding more yellow than blue to make a yellowish-green.

Color Collage

Materials: a variety of colorful magazines

Choose one of your favorite color themes. Using the color you have chosen, create a collage out of magazine pictures that contain different hues or shades of your color.

Easel Painting

Materials: art supplies; easels

Set up an easel with tempera paints. Paint a picture of your choosing, making it as colorful as possible.

Finger Painting

Materials: cookie sheets; finger painting supplies

Place a sheet of finger-painting paper on the cookie sheet. Dampen the paper with water and add paint. Explore, dabble, swirl, and create with colors and shapes.

Bodily/Kinesthetic

Creating Rainbows

Materials: mirror; drinking glass; flashlight

Fill a glass with water and place it and a mirror in front of a window. Arrange them so that the sun will shine through the glass of water and onto the mirror. Turn the glass and/or the mirror until you see a rainbow appear on the wall or on the ceiling. As you turn the glass and the mirror, the rainbow will change in size and in the number of colors displayed. Record the changes the rainbow makes as you turn the glass and mirror. You may also want to try using a flashlight in place of the sun.

Get Twisted

Materials: skill cards; a Twister game mat or any mat with eight colored circles

Working with a partner, take turns asking one another quetions and getting twisted. Ask your partner a question. If he or she answers it correctly, you may tell the person to place a hand or foot on any color you choose. Continue asking questions until you succeed in making your partner tumble over. Switch roles.

Create a Character

Materials: a collection of different colored hats; art and writing materials

Look through the collection of hats and pick one that you would like to create for a character. Put the hat on and think about the character who would wear this hat. Draw or write about your character and why he or she would wear a hat of that particular color.

Logical/Mathematical

Counters of Many Colors

Materials: a variety of colorful counters

Use your imagination to make a variety of colorful patterns out of counters. On a worksheet (see fig. 10.1), write the patterns you have created.

Counters of Many Colors

1. Example: A A B A A B A A B	2.
3.	4.
5.	6.
7.	8.

Figure 10.1

Musical/Rhythmic

Rhythms of Color

Materials: cassette player; a variety of music tapes

Listen to a variety of music selections. As you listen to each selection, think about how the music makes you feel and what color represents that feeling to you. Then, fill in the box for that selection with that color (see fig. 10.2).

Streamer Beat

Materials: cassette player; a variety of music tapes; long streamers of colored crepe paper or ribbons

As you listen to a song, think about how it makes you feel. Choose a color of paper or ribbon that fits your mood and move with the beat. If you like, dance with more than one color.

Picture Sounds

Materials: art supplies; cassette player; a tape with sounds of different places such as a farm, city, countryside, night, or rain forest

Listen to the sounds on the tape and, using paints, markers, or crayons, draw colorful pictures

Rhythms of Color

1	2	3	4
5	6	7	8

Figure 10.2

inspired by the sounds you hear. You can draw either realistic scenes or simply your impressions of colors.

Interpersonal

Things in Our Colored World

With a partner, brainstorm the colors of everything you have. Consider items such as clothes, toys, pictures on the walls of your room. Record the results of your brainstorming on a chart (see fig. 10.3).

Next, make a graph of the items you and your partner chose. How many different colors do you have? How many colors are the same?

Finally, ask your friends what their favorite colors are. Graph the data. You may also want to ask them why they chose the color they did.

Intrapersonal

Rainbows of Color

Materials: art supplies

Draw a large rainbow. Think about each of the colors and then, in the rainbow, write something about yourself that each of the colors symbolizes for you.

Things in Our Colored World

Name: _____

Orange	Red	Green	Blue
Brown	Purple	Yellow	Black

Figure 10.3

Colors of Your Week

Think about the past week and what you did and how you felt during the morning and after-noon of each day. Choose a color that represents to you each of those feelings and color in the appropriate boxes (see fig. 10.4). The labels for the boxes could be morning/evening or school/after school.

Colors of Your Week

	Sunday	Monday	Tuesday	Wednesday	Thursday	Friday	Saturday
A.M.							
P.M.							

Figure 10.4

IRI/Skylight Training and Publishing, Inc.

Other Ideas for Colors of Our World Centers

Unit of focus: _____

Verbal/Linguistic:	Musical/Rhythmic:
Logical/Mathematical:	Visual/Spatial:
Bodily/Kinesthetic:	Intrapersonal:
Interpersonal:	Arrangement Tips:

Figure 10.5

IRI/Skylight Training and Publishing, Inc.

Centers for Colors of Our World:
My Plan for Implementation

Unit of focus: _____

Targeted Intelligence:	Targeted Intelligence:
Materials:	Materials:
Task:	Task:
Targeted Intelligence:	Targeted Intelligence:
Materials:	Materials:
Task:	Task:
Targeted Intelligence:	Targeted Intelligence:
Materials:	Materials:
Task:	Task:
Targeted Intelligence:	Targeted Intelligence:
Materials:	Materials:
Task:	Task:

Figure 10.6

IRI/Skylight Training and Publishing, Inc.

■ *Projects*

Verbal/Linguistic

A Coat of Many Colors

Research the different ways that animals use color for survival. You may want to consider adaptations such as mimicry or camouflage. After you have completed your research, write a booklet that illustrates and explains how color can protect animals. Title your booklet "A Coat of Many Colors." You may want to consider using illustrations in your booklet.

Tickled Pink

Choose eight people who are "tickled pink" about something they have accomplished. Create a large flipbook and on the bottom of each page, write the individual's name. You may want to consider individuals such as Michael Jordan, Superman, Abraham Lincoln, Barney, your principal, one of your teachers, Betsy Ross, Harriet Tubman, Martin Luther King Jr., or Whitney Houston. Then think about what accomplishment each individual is tickled pink about. Illustrate the accomplishment in the blank space above the individual's name. Write the accomplishment on the back of the page. Your flipbook can now be used in a "Guess What I'm Tickled Pink About?" quiz that you play with your classmates. Make sure your pictures are challenging.

Visual/Spatial

My Favorite Color

Select one of your favorite colors and collect twenty to twenty-four pictures (they can be photographs you have taken, drawings, or pictures from magazines) that demonstrate a variety of ways you have discovered this color in your surroundings. Look at nature, houses, billboards, flower beds, vehicles, etc. When you have collected all your images, compile a picture essay that tells your story of this color.

Artistic Style

Learn about an artist by investigating how he or she uses color. Examine the use of color in a variety of his or her paintings, and think about how choosing other colors would have affected the style of the paintings. When you have finished studying the artist's works, choose one of the paintings and paint your own version of it. Decide whether you want to use the same colors as the artist used. Be prepared to explain how you used color to portray the artist's style. Compare your painting to the painting you copied.

Musical/Rhythmic

The Color of Joy

Read all or part of *Hailstone and the Halibut Bones* by Mary O'Neill, a book that explores the colors of various emotions. Invent a song that uses color to describe and tell about yourself and how you feel about various things. Use a familiar tune such as "Battle Hymn of the Republic" to accompany your lyrics.

Am I Blue?

Think about how colors can be associated with sounds and emotions. Choose six to eight emotions to choreograph using rhythmic sounds and a variety of colors. Next, select several pieces of music that best suit the emotions you have chosen and record them on tape. Create masks of different colors to represent each of the emotions and the accompanying music you have chosen. Present your selections to the class. Wear one of the colored masks and panto-mime the emotion to your music selection. Music and drama will bring your colors to life.

Bodily/Kinesthetic

Nature Collage

Go on a nature hunt and gather a variety of objects that display the colors of the current season. (Doing this project in the wintertime can be challenging.) Create a collage with the colors and the objects you found. The finished product should be titled, mounted, and framed for display. Include a list of all the materials you used.

Colors in Motion

Make eight to ten paper or fabric streamers of different colors. Select several thirty-second segments of music. Use the streamers to choreograph a visual display of movement that shows how each color might move to the beat. Be sure to match the tempo of your selections to the colors you have chosen.

Seasonal Animals

Choose an animal and research how it adapts to the changing seasons of its habitat. Explore how the animal is affected by its color and the colors of the seasons. Make a diorama representing the four seasons of your animal's habitat. Label each season and show how your animal adapts its lifestyle patterns during that time of the year.

Logical/Mathematical

Create a Color

Invent several formulas that can be used to create three new colors. Start with tempera or acrylic paint in the primary and secondary colors and experiment with your formulas. Make sure they can be duplicated. Give your new colors names and choose one to be used for a new product promotion that you will advertise and display. Keep in mind that some colors do not work well with some products. For example, blue is rarely used when advertising food products. This color seems to make people lose their appetite.

Weaving In and Out

Use color to weave a pattern. Materials used for the project can vary from plastic lacing, rope, and yarn to raffia, paper, or reeds. Research the process of weaving and familiarize yourself with the warp, or "spokes," and the weft, or "weavers." The coiling method of weaving can also be used. Weave your color pattern and repeat it until the project is completed. Your final product can be a basket, a belt, a headband, a placemat, etc. Display your finished product and be prepared to explain the art of weaving the materials you used and how you planned your color pattern.

Math Tessellations

Research and apply the study of tessellations to the use of color and art in the geometry of polygons. After familiarizing yourself with the definition of a regular polygon (all sides equal in length and all angles congruent), investigate which polygons tessellate. Use sponge printing to create four tessellations using different patterns of colors and polygons. The tessellated patterns should extend in all directions to completely cover an 18 x 18-inch plane without leaving any gaps.

Interpersonal

Family Colors

Working in groups of four to five, research the characteristics of color. Discuss how a color wheel is like a family and how the individual colors are like the members of a family. Decide which color best represents each person in your group (e.g., most colorful, warmest color, coolest color, etc.). Does your group include primary colors as well as secondary colors? Are complementary colors represented in your group? Have each member of your group display their colors by listing the ways color is used to symbolize and unite people. For example, red, white, and blue represent the United States flag and the United States in general.

Have your group come up with nineteen to twenty-five samples of "showing our colors" and present them to the class. You can show your group's colors using drawings, slogans, poems, and/or pictures cut out of magazines.

What's My Color

Research the color analysis services used by fashion consultants to advise individuals which colors, based on the seasons, are the most complimentary for them to wear. Based on your research, provide your own consulting service for eight to ten of your peers. Record and gather information you need to perform your color analysis. Include hair color, skin tone, eye color, etc. Present your findings and recommendations. Include samples of the colors you have chosen for each of your "clients." Ask your clients for a reaction to your recommendations.

Intrapersonal

Green with Envy

Investigate the psychology of color and explore how colors affect our different moods and emotions. List ten to fifteen colorful facts you discovered. An example of a color fact is "red denotes power." Choose ten to twelve of the color facts you discovered and use examples to create a "Color Me" booklet that explains what effects your colors can have on people. For example, "Fact: Red is a sign of power." Businessmen sometimes wear red ties to important meetings, or, red is often used in symbols and signs of the Communist party.

Color Smart

Familiarize yourself with the multiple intelligences identified by Howard Gardner. Choose different colors of fabric swatches to represent each of the multiple intelligences. Think about why you chose each of these colors. Be prepared to display your color swatches and explain the intelligence each represents. Enhance your presentation by wearing an article of clothing that goes with each intelligence and matches the color you selected for that intelligence. For example, wear a blue headband to represent the logical/mathematical intelligence and red tights/leotard to represent the musical/rhythmic intelligence.

CHAPTER
11

Creepy Critters

The centers and projects in this chapter are designed to help teach any science unit that incorporates the study of insects in general, and the study of ants in particular. After the students understand the definition of an insect, they can apply the scientific skill of observation to study insect classification, habitat, morphology, prey, predators, and adaptations.

The centers and projects that follow are designed to integrate the study of insects through targeted multiple intelligences. Students will use literature, science facts, and music to guide them in a variety of creative and problem-solving tasks. For example, literature is incorporated into the Ant Adventures project, while music plays a key role in the Bug Jive center and the I Think I Can, I Think I Can project. These center activities and projects will enrich and supplement any aspect of insect study.

■ Centers

Verbal/Linguistic

Cards of Center Ant-ology

Materials: a variety of cards with questions and/or prompts such as those shown in figure 11.1; answer sheets

Increase your knowledge about insects by drawing a card and writing your answer on an answer sheet. When your answer sheet is filled, create your own Center Ant-ology question cards and continue playing the game.

Rhyme Lime

Materials: writing supplies

Create a rhyming poem that shows off what you know about ants. Here is a first verse to get you started:

>   I have two—an ant has six,
>
>   Our cool legs can do neat tricks.
>
>   With a crawl, hop, jump, leap, and skip,
>
>   This little insect made quite a trip.

Add to the poem by creating a verse for either the ant's nose, eyes, size, adventures, and/or antennae, etc.

Visual/Spatial

Critter Field Study

Materials: writing and drawing supplies

Learn more about insects by creating a tiny book of critters using one of the following approaches:

1. Draw a picture of your critter; include its name (scientific and common).

2. Write facts about your critters such as:

Homes	Way They Travel	Body Coverings	Foods They Eat	Stages of Life	Benefits to People

Ant-ology Cards

Three words to describe an ant.	Why an ant would (or would not) want to exchange places with you.	Three things an ant can do that you can't.
Plan an ant lunch menu. Name three things that you and the ant share and three things the ant wouldn't care for.	Three parts of an ant's body.	What do you do with your teeth that an ant does with its mandibles?
How are an ant's antennae and your nose alike.	An ant thinks like a ___, moves like a ___, and eats like a ___.	How are your eyes different from an ant's?
Suggest one word that best describes your world and the ant world.	WILD CARD! Make up your own question.	Write four things that bug you.

Figure 11.1

IRI/Skylight Training and Publishing, Inc.

Doodle Bugs

Materials: cards or a chart that lists bugs with descriptive names, such as firefly, fire ant, and ladybug; art supplies

Draw a card or choose a name from the chart. Use your imagination and what you know about bugs to create, draw, and name an imaginary bug with a similar name. For example, if you chose firefly, you might want to invent a firespider.

Geobugs

Materials: various geometric shapes, such as pattern blocks

Create a variety of imaginary and realistic insects using geometric shapes.

Symmetry

Materials: art supplies; Mylar mirrors

Fold a piece of paper in half. Along the fold of the paper, draw an outline of one side of an insect. Cut out your insect, unfold the paper, and admire its symmetry. Think about what other insects look like and whether they are symmetric. In other words, if you draw a line from their top to their bottom, are the two sides mirror images of each other? You can also use a Mylar mirror to demonstrate symmetry. Draw the right or left half of an insect. Hold your drawing up to the mirror. Can you see the complete insect?

Bodily/Kinesthetic

Down on the Farm

Materials: empty two-liter plastic bottles; plastic aquarium tubing; sand; ants; rubber or cork stoppers

Increase your knowledge of the life of an ant by building and observing an ant farm. Add sand to the bottles and connect them using plastic tubing (see fig. 11.2). Introduce the ants to their new home. Make sure all the bottles are securely plugged so your ants don't escape. Don't forget to supply your ants with food and water.

Observe the ants as they explore their new home. Do they prefer one bottle over another? Log your findings in a class log. Include your name, the time, and any unusual observations. Other students can continue to log observations. Look at the log after a week or two to see how your ants have adjusted to their new home.

Ant Journey

Materials: a variety of objects such as rocks, feathers, glass

Choose one of the objects and touch and examine it. Now close your eyes and imagine you are

Down on the Farm

Figure 11.2

an ant and have encountered this object on your quest for food. Draw or write an "ant journey," describing what the ant would see or feel while making its way across the object you have chosen. Don't forget to consider the size of the ant in relation to the object.

Logical/Mathematical

Critter Races

Materials: earthworms, caterpillars, or any other crawling critter; stopwatch

Working with a partner, pick two crawling critters and have a race. Mark one with an ink spot. Put each contestant on a spot on a piece of paper marked with an X. As the critters start to crawl, mark their paths with a pencil. Let them crawl for one minute and note how they move. Measure each of their paths. The winning critter is the one that crawled the farthest. Record your data in a class log. After the whole class has visited the center, compare the distances your critters crawled.

Ant Exploration

Materials: a variety of small objects such as pine cones, sea shells, rocks, buttons, etc.

Touch and examine each object and match your findings with its characteristics (e.g., pine cone—sticky, barbed, round, prickly, smooth, curved, bumpy). Come up with as many adjectives as you can for each object.

Critter Collection

Materials: insect reference books

Collect as many critters as you can and place each one in a separate Ziploc bag. The more critters you have, the better. Look at your collection and learn about the different types of insects by sorting and classifying them according to their differences and their similarities. Look at a reference book to help you with your classification.

Critter Wheels

Use a Venn diagram to compare two insects of your choice. Consider characteristics such as size, color, habitat, ability to fly, etc. Record your findings in the Venn diagram (see fig. 11.3). When you are done, repeat the comparison using three insects (see fig. 11.4). Find which attributes all three insects share and those that only two share. Do any of your critters have a unique characteristic?

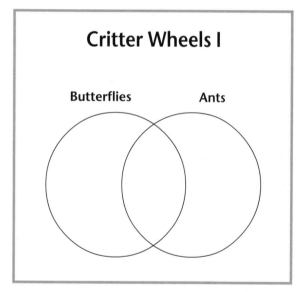

Figure 11.3

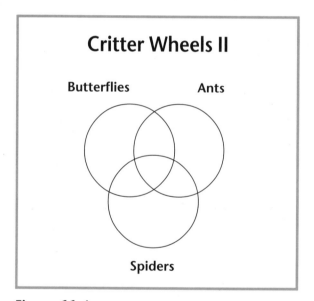

Figure 11.4

Touchy T

Explore the characteristics of insects by using a T-chart (see fig. 11.5). Choose one of your favorite critters. Think about what it looks like, sounds like, and feels like. Record your findings in the chart. Repeat this with several other insects and compare their T-charts.

Musical/Rhythmic

Bug Jive

Materials: cassette player; headphones; a variety of music selections

Touchy T

Looks Like . . .	Sounds Like . . .	Feels Like . . .

Figure 11.5

Choose a partner and assign the names A and B. A is the leader and listens to a variety of music using headphones. A then tries to imagine how a creepy crawler would move to the music and starts to dance. B then attempts to mirror A's movements. After five or ten minutes, swap roles.

Eating Critters

Materials: writing supplies

Write a poem or a song using one of the following lines as a first verse. Recall how people feel about a particular insect or animal.

Susie Squiron ate a worm . . .

Billy Bake ate a snake . . .

Julie Jider ate a spider . . .

Danny Dizzard ate a lizard . . .

Jamie Jee ate a flea . . .

Interpersonal

Graphing Creeps

Materials: large Post-it notes

Working in a group of three to five, brainstorm a list of different kinds of insects. Write the name of each insect at the top of a large Post-it note and divide the note into "yes" and "no" columns. Now, let everyone think about each insect and decide whether or not they would allow it to crawl on their hands. Record and graph the group's findings (see fig. 11.6). Which insects were the winners and which were the losers? Can you think of some reasons why?

Graphing Creeps

Spider		Caterpillar		Butterfly		Ant		Roach		Fly	
Yes	No	Yes	No	Yes	No	Yes	No	Yes	No	Yes	No

Figure 11.6

IRI/Skylight Training and Publishing, Inc.

Cooperative Antics

Have you ever noticed that an ant is almost never alone? In a small group, brainstorm ways ants work together. Record your findings on a chart. Now, brainstorm ways that people work together and record those findings on the chart. Compare the two (see fig. 11.7).

To better visualize how people work together and ants work together, transfer the findings from your chart to a Venn diagram. How did you work together on this project? (see fig. 11.8)

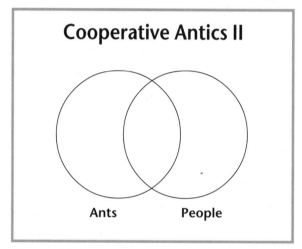

Cooperative Antics I	
Ants work together by	We work together by

Figure 11.7

Figure 11.8

Intrapersonal

Microbug

Materials: clear tape; several insect specimens; index cards

Create an insect collection that is easy to view. Cut a hole in the center of an index card. Place a piece of clear tape over the hole. Place a specimen on the sticky side of the tape. Add another piece of tape to seal in your specimen. Label the index card with the name of the insect. Refer to these cards any time you want to study an insect up close.

Buggy Thoughts

Materials: writing supplies

Think about insect behavior you have observed and studied. Then, write about one of the following:

1. Something that drives you "buggy."

2. "Antics" that people do.

3. If I were a bug, I would . . . .

Other Ideas for Creepy Critters Centers

Unit of focus: _____

Verbal/Linguistic:	**Musical/Rhythmic:**
Logical/Mathematical:	**Visual/Spatial:**
Bodily/Kinesthetic:	**Intrapersonal:**
Interpersonal:	**Arrangement Tips:**

Figure 11.9

IRI/Skylight Training and Publishing, Inc.

Centers for Creepy Critters:
My Plan for Implementation

Unit of focus: _____

Targeted Intelligence: Materials: Task:	Targeted Intelligence: Materials: Task:
Targeted Intelligence: Materials: Task:	Targeted Intelligence: Materials: Task:
Targeted Intelligence: Materials: Task:	Targeted Intelligence: Materials: Task:
Targeted Intelligence: Materials: Task:	Targeted Intelligence: Materials: Task:

Figure 11.10

IRI/Skylight Training and Publishing, Inc.

■ Projects

Verbal/Linguistic

Ant Adventures

Two Bad Ants by Chris Van Allsburg is an example of a story written from an ant's point of view. Write a creative story or poem of your own about the obstacles that two bad ants encountered one day in your school. Make sure your ants encounter at least six obstacles and that they learn some kind of a lesson. Your story should be in booklet form and the obstacles should be illustrated from the ant's perspective, just as they are in Chris Van Allsburg's story.

Pesty Critters

Select, research, and write about four to six insect pests that are harmful to humans. Think about which pests are merely an inconvenience and which are truly harmful. Which pests destroy property or crops and transmit diseases? Also, consider which home remedies or pest control services appear effective in controlling these pesty insects. Rate the pests you have chosen from the most harmful to the least harmful.

Visual/Spatial

Ant-thology

Refer to a few pages of *Antics,* an ABC book by Cathi Hepworth, for inspiration. Brainstorm as many words as you can that have the letters a-n-t in them. You may have to consult a dictionary for words and definitions. Create your own ant-thology. Include your words, their definitions, and an illustration of each word.

A Is for Ant

Create an ant picture dictionary of words that would be meaningful in an ant's life. You do not need to have a word for every letter of the alphabet. Alphabetically list your words on separate pages. Each word should be placed at the bottom of the page; the top of the page should contain an illustration of the word drawn from an ant's perspective (pretend you are an ant looking up at the object).

The Search Is On

Pretend you are an ant crawling through your house in search of a tasty treat. Imagine where you would enter the house and where the treat is located. Do you have any pets that the ant might encounter? Would the ant's path to its treat cross any dangerous heavy-traffic areas in your house? Map out the floor plan of your house, showing the path the ant would take. Indicate any special obstacles and danger spots your ant would have to pass.

Bodily/Kinesthetic

Insect Museum

Make and display an insect collection. Collect eight to ten different insects and label each insect by number. Use a box to display your collection. Create a small field guide whose page numbers correspond to each numbered insect. Include the following information in the guide:

1. Common name of insect
2. Scientific name of insect
3. Distinguishing physical features
4. Life span and birth statistics
5. Eating habits
6. Interesting facts

Logical/Mathematical

Anthletes and Arthropods

Using baseball cards as a model, make twenty to thirty oversized sports cards from tagboard. Place a picture of an insect on the front and its preferred sport on the back, along with the following statistics:

1. Common Name
2. Scientific Name
3. Size
4. Physical Characteristics
5. Eating Habits
6. Interesting Facts

Create a game using your insect sports cards.

Crosswords

Create a "Tunnel of Ant Trivia" crossword puzzle. List twenty-four interesting vocabulary words associated with the study of ants. Put at least twenty of the words into a crossword pattern. Create challenging clues to match your words. Hand out copies of the crossword puzzle to the class. When you turn in your completed crossword project, include the answer sheet.

Musical/Rhythmic

Buzzing Out

Working in a group of four or five students, brainstorm a variety of insect sounds. Think about places where you have heard insect sounds, such as in a field on a hot summer day. Or, you just might want to come up with your own insect combination. Select insects your group will mimic. Each individual will make one insect's sound. Practice in unison. Orchestrate and perform your selection.

The Beetles?

In a small group, design and make instruments that simulate insect sounds. Consider including several types of instruments, such as wind, percussion, and string. Either make up your own song or play a favorite tune. When you have practiced your selection several times, perform it for the class.

I Think I Can, I Think I Can

Try to remember a time when you encountered an insurmountable obstacle and yet you eventually overcame it. Then, using the lyrics and the tune from "High Hopes" as an inspiration, write a song that tells about your obstacle and how humor helped you overcome your problem. Record your song on tape and play it for the class.

Interpersonal

News Ants Can Use

We know that ants communicate and work well together. Now is your chance to show your cooperative skills as part of a four-member ant news team that works on "Nightly News with Pet Ant Jennings." Have your team cover at least five interesting "antivities" from around the world. Here are some ideas:

1. Some ants have captured smaller ants and are keeping them as slaves. One ant prisoner recently escaped from enemy territory.

2. Movie and entertainment reviews for ants.

3. Army ant invasions around the world.

4. Ants spend a lot of time cleaning and grooming themselves. Advertise some beauty products for ants.

5. Present the latest "Ant Delectables" created to look like ants. Provide recipes for your ant food.

6. New colonies are being established by newly formed political leaders. Each fledgling colony has its own flag.

If possible, videotape your newscast.

Mission Possible

With a partner, create a training manual for teaching ant recruits how to attack and devour food on a picnic table without interference from their human enemy. As general of the army ants boot camp, you and your partner will need to develop six strategies that will conquer and divide the interfering humans.

Intrapersonal

Social Antics

Ants devote every day of their lives to caring for one another, working together, and protecting members of the colony from harm. These social insects exhibit close companionship. Humans live in family units and form friendships with those outside their family.

Write about a special friendship you share with someone. Think of qualities you have identified in ants that are equally important in human relationships. Describe your friend and what you admire about him or her, how long you have known each other, and a special experience you shared. End your oral presentation by explaining what makes your friendship strong.

Save the Ant?

Should humans be responsible for protecting the life of ants? Do you think it is OK to destroy ants? If we destroyed half of the ants in this country, would the ecosystem be harmed? Is our ecosystem harmed when we kill all the ants in our own backyard? Should humans protect the ants' habitat? Write a pamphlet that supports your opinion. Use facts to back up your position.

Afterword

Howard Gardner has recently suggested the possibility of an eighth intelligence—the naturalist intelligence. Individuals with a strength in this intelligence can recognize and distinguish between and among a variety of species of plants and animals, as well as make other distinctions and categorizations in "nature" (Gardner 1995). Historical figures with a strength in this intelligence include Charles Darwin and John James Audubon. Other individuals with this intelligence would include "experts" such as wildlife biologists, entomologists, and Aleutian hunters, and "novices" such as gardeners and the youngster who is able to distinguish easily among a dozen different kinds of dinosaurs. Although the term naturalist suggests "rural" explorations, it applies just as well to "urban" ones, as expressed by youngsters who can distinguish readily among a wide variety of makes and models of cars.

After reviewing the sample centers and projects found in Section 2, as well as the exploratory centers and the Picture-Essay project in Section 1, it will be evident that the naturalist intelligence supports a number of centers and projects. For example, consider the following, found in Chapter Seven, "Discoveries of the Deep Oceans": Cartoon Sharks and Sharkmobiles projects and Sea Murals, Fish Kites, and Sea Songs centers. All of these activities have a strong supporting naturalist intelligence, which could be transformed easily into the targeted intelligence by making slight changes in the objectives and the emphasis.

Several of the activities in the "Creepy Critters" chapter also have a strong supporting naturalist intelligence.

Although less obvious, the Artistic Style project and the Streamer Beat center found in Chapter Ten, "Colors of Our World," also reflect the naturalist intelligence. In this case we see the "urban" variety, exploring the differentiation among and categorization of the artistic use of color and musical rhythms, respectively.

Finally, we are including a suggestion for an exploratory center and a project, which can be used in the "Colors of Our World" unit of study.

Naturalist Exploratory Center

Supply this center with a variety of collections that the students can view and explore as they learn to note the differences and similarities among the items studied. Examples include: leaves, rocks, seashells, wildflowers, insects, and animal skins. Magnifying glasses, rulers, and reference books such as field guides to trees or insects will help the students with their classifications.

Falling Leaves Project

Research a variety of deciduous trees, paying particular attention to their leaves and the changing colors as winter approaches. In the fall, collect the leaves of at least fifteen different species of trees and determine how color helps you in their identification. Create a collection of your leaves. Iron them on low heat between wax paper and mount them on paper or cardboard. For each specimen in your collection, identify at least two characteristics that distinguish that leaf from all the others and include a comment on the role that color played in your identification.

Experiment with ideas of your own as you consider the many possibilities of the naturalist intelligence.

IRI/Skylight Training and Publishing, Inc.

Appendix A

Junk Box Item Suggestions

Stock your junk box with some of the following materials. The junk box can constitute a center in itself or it can be used in a variety of other center activities or projects.

- [ ] spools
- [ ] beads and buttons
- [ ] corks
- [ ] pill, cologne, and other small, empty bottles
- [ ] jugs and other plastic bottles
- [ ] cardboard tubes from toilet tissue and paper towels
- [ ] paper towels
- [ ] kitchen plastic wrap
- [ ] wrapping paper
- [ ] old socks and nylon stockings
- [ ] magazines
- [ ] gift cards
- [ ] tissue paper
- [ ] paper bags of all sizes

☐ egg cartons

☐ twigs

☐ seashells

☐ assorted rocks and pebbles

☐ plastic containers

☐ scraps of fabric

☐ packing materials

☐ string, yarn, ribbon

☐ lids and jar tops

The following foods can also be included in the junk box:

☐ dried beans

☐ pasta

☐ rice

☐ dry cereal

☐ seeds

Appendix B

An Assortment of Recipes

The following collection of recipes can be used with any number of project or center activities. It is suggested that the teacher prepare the recipes for student use.

Salt Paint

2/3 c. salt

pinch of cornstarch

$^1/_2$ tsp. food coloring

Spread on cookie sheet or wax paper to dry. Put in large-holed salt shaker for use.

Soap Paint

3 c. powdered laundry detergent

$1^1/_2$ c. hot water

Mix and whip with egg beater until stiff. Use immediately. (This works great for snow scenes.)

Sand Paint

1 c. sifted dry sand

2 Tbs. tempera paint

Mix together. To use, brush paper with watered-down glue
where you want to use the sand paint. Shake paint on the wet
surface.

Soap Bubbles

1 c. water

2 tsp. liquid detergent

½ tsp. sugar

1 tsp. glycerin

Mix and use immediately. Bubble pipes can be made out of pipe
cleaners.

No-Cook Play Dough

2 c. self-rising flour

2 Tbs. alum

2 Tbs. salt

2 Tbs. cooking oil

$1\frac{1}{4}$ c. boiling water

Mix, knead, and store in an air-tight container. A little food coloring can be added if desired.

Cooked Play Dough

1 c. flour

$\frac{1}{2}$ c. salt

1 c. water

1 Tbs. cooking oil

2 tsp. cream of tarter

Mix and heat until ingredients form a ball. Add a little food coloring if desired.

Papier-Mâché

Mix equal parts of liquid starch and water. Stir until the starch dissolves. Soak newspaper strips in the liquid mixture and use immediately.

Bibliography

Allsburg, C. V. 1988. *Two bad ants.* Boston: Houghton Mifflin.

America Online Aviation Forum, World Wide Web. Dr. James Marden's home page (http: //cac. psu. edu/ jhm10/).

Andron, S. 1990. *In quest of solutions to the mysteries inside.* Mobile, Ala.: GCT Publications.

Armstrong, T. 1993. *Seven kinds of smart: Identifying and developing your many intelligences.* New York: Penguin Books.

Atwood, Margaret. 1995. *Princess Prunella and the purple peanut.* New York: Workman Publishing.

Barrett, S. L. 1992. *It's all in your head: A guide to understanding your brain and boosting your brain power.* Minneapolis, Minn.: Free Spirit Publishing.

Bellanca, J., and R. Fogarty. 1990. *Blueprints for thinking in the cooperative classroom.* Palatine, Ill.: IRI/Skylight Training and Publishing.

Berman, S. 1993. *Catch them thinking in science: A handbook of classroom strategies.* Palatine, Ill.: IRI/Skylight Training and Publishing.

———. 1995. *A multiple intelligences road to a quality classroom.* Palatine, Ill.: IRI/Skylight Training and Publishing.

Blythe, T., and H. Gardner. 1990. A school for all intelligences. *Educational Leadership,* April, 33–37.

Boulding, E. 1966. *The image.* Ann Arbor: University of Michigan Press.

Britton, J., and W. Britton. 1992. *Teaching tessellating art—Activities and transparency masters.* Palo Alto, Calif.: Dale Seymour Publications.

Burke, K. 1992. *What to do with the kid who . . . : Developing cooperation, self-discipline, and responsibility in the classroom.* Palatine, Ill.: IRI/Skylight Training and Publishing.

———. 1995. *Managing the interactive classroom: A collection of articles.* Palatine, Ill.: IRI/Skylight Training and Publishing.

Buzan, T. 1977. *Use both sides of your brain.* Richardson, Tex.: Magnamusic-Baton.

Caine, R., and G. Caine. 1990. Understanding a brain-based approach to learning and teaching. *Educational Leadership,* October, 66–70.

———. 1991. *Making connections: Teaching and the human brain.* Alexandria, Va.: Association for Supervision and Curriculum Development.

Campbell, J. 1989. *The improbable machine: What the new upheavals in artifical intelligence research reveal about how the mind really works.* New York: Simon & Schuster.

———. 1992. *Teaching and learning through multiple intelligences.* Seattle: New Horizons for Learning.

———. 1994. *The multiple intelligences handbook.* Stanwood, Wash.: Campbell and Associates, Inc.

Carr, E., and D. Ogle. 1987. K-W-L Plus: A strategy for comprehension and summarization. *Journal of Reading,* 30(7): 626–31.

Ceci, J. 1990. *On intelligence—More or less: A bio-ecological treatise in intellectual development.* Englewood Cliffs, N.J.: Prentice Hall.

Chapman, C. 1993. *If the shoe fits . . . : How to develop multiple intelligences in the classroom.* Palatine, Ill.: IRI/Skylight Training and Publishing.

Common miracles: The new American revolution in learning. 1993. Produced by D. Guilbalt and directed by G. Paul. 50 min. MPI Home Video. Videocassette.

Costa, A. L. 1991a. Fostering intelligent behavior. *On the beam.* Vol 7. Seattle: New Horizons for Learning.

———. 1991b. *The school as a home for the mind.* Palatine, Ill.: IRI/Skylight Training and Publishing.

———, ed. 1985. *Developing minds.* Alexandria, Va.: Association for Supervision and Curriculum Development.

Costa, A., J. Bellanca, and R. Fogarty. 1992a. *If minds matter: A foreword to the future.* Vol. 1. Palatine, Ill.: IRI/Skylight Training and Publishing.

———. 1992b. *If minds matter: A foreword to the future.* Vol. 2. Palatine, Ill.: IRI/Skylight Training and Publishing.

Csikszentmihalyi, M. 1990. *Flow: The psychology of optimal experience.* New York: Harper & Row.

deBono, E. 1985. *Six thinking hats.* Boston: Little, Brown.

————. 1992. *Serious creativity: Using the power for lateral thinking to create new ideas.* New York: HarperCollins Publishers, Inc.

Dickinson, D. 1987. *New development in cognitive research.* Seattle: New Horizons for Learning.

Faculty of the New City School. 1994. *Celebrating multiple intelligences: Teaching for success.* St. Louis, Mo.: The New City School, Inc.

Feldman, D. H. 1986. *Nature's Gambit: Child prodigies and the development of human potential.* New York: Basic Books.

Feuerstein, R. 1980. *Instrumental Enrichment.* Baltimore: University Park Press.

Feuerstein, R., Y. Rand, M. B. Hoffman, and R. Miller. 1980. *Instrumental Enrichment: An intervention program for cognitive modifiability.* Baltimore: University Park Press.

Fogarty, R. 1991. *The mindful school: How to integrate the curricula.* Palatine, Ill.: IRI/Skylight Training and Publishing.

————. 1995a. *Best practices for the learner-centered classroom.* Palatine, Ill.: IRI/Skylight Training and Publishing.

————, ed. 1995b. *Think about . . . Multiage classrooms.* Palatine, Ill.: IRI/Skylight Training and Publishing.

Fogarty, R., and J. Bellanca. 1986. *Catch them thinking: A handbook of classroom strategies.* Palatine, Ill.: IRI/Skylight Training and Publishing.

————. 1986. *Teach Them Thinking: Mental menus for 24 thinking skills.* Palatine, Ill.: IRI/Skylight Training and Publishing.

————. 1989. *Patterns for thinking: Patterns for transfer.* Palatine, Ill.: IRI/Skylight Training and Publishing.

————, eds. 1995. *Multiple intelligences: A collection.* Palatine, Ill.: IRI/Skylight Training and Publishing.

Fogarty, R., D. Perkins, and J. Barell. 1992. *The mindful school: How to teach for transfer.* Palatine, Ill.: IRI/Skylight Training and Publishing.

Fogarty, R., and J. Stoehr. 1995. *Integrating curricula with multiple intelligences: Teams, themes, and threads.* Palatine, Ill.: IRI/Skylight Training and Publishing.

Fowler, C. 1990. Recognizing the role of artistic intelligences. *Music Educators Journal* 77(1): 24–27.

Gardner, H. 1983. *Frames of mind: The theory of multiple intelligences.* New York: Basic Books.

————. 1987a. The theory of multiple intelligences. *Annals of Dyslexia* 37, 19–35.

————. 1987b. Developing the spectrum of human intelligences: Teaching in the eighties, a need to change. *Harvard Educational Review* 57, 187–93.

————. 1993. *Multiple intelligences: The theory in practice.* New York: HarperCollins.

————. 1995. Reflections on multiple intelligences: Myths and messages. *Phi Delta Kappan,* November, 200–209.

Gardner, H., and T. Hatch. 1989. Multiple intelligences go to school: Educational implications of the theory of multiple intelligences. *Educational Researcher* 18(8): 14–19.

Gardner, H., and T. Hatch. 1990. *Multiple intelligences go to school: Educational implications of the theory of multiple intelligences (Report No. 4).* New York: Center for Technology in Education.

Gawain, S. 1978. *Creative visualization.* New York: Bantam Books.

Glasser, W. 1986. *Control theory in the classroom.* New York: Harper & Row.

————. 1990. *The quality school.* New York: Harper, Perennial.

Golden, D., and A. Tsiaras. 1994. Building a better brain. *Life,* July, 62–71.

Haggerty, B. A. 1995. *Nurturing intelligences: A guide to multiple intelligences theory and teaching.* White Plains, New York: Addison-Wesley Publishing.

Hammerman, E., and D. Musial. *Classroom 2061: Activity-based assessments in science integrated with mathematics and language arts.* Palatine, Ill.: IRI/Skylight Training and Publishing.

Harman, W. 1988. *The global mind change.* Indianapolis: Knowledge Systems.

Harman, W., and H. Reingold. 1985. *Higher creativity.* Los Angeles: J. P. Tarcher.

Johnson, D., and R. Johnson. 1987. *Learning together and alone: Cooperative, competitive, and individualistic learning.* Englewood Cliffs, N.J.: Prentice Hall.

Jones, B. F., A. Palincsar, D. S. Ogle, and E. G. Carr. 1987. *Strategic teaching and learning: Cognitive instruction in the content areas.* Alexandria, Va.: Association for Supervision and Curriculum Development.

Kagan, S. 1992. *Cooperative learning.* San Juan Capistrano, Calif.: Resources for Teachers, Inc.

Machado, L. 1980. *The right to be intelligent.* New York: Pergamon Press.

Mason, K. 1991. *Going beyond words: The art and practice of visual thinking.* Tucson: Zephyr Press.

Miller, L. 1990. The roles of language and learning in the development of literacy. *Topics in Language Disorders* 10(2): 1–24.

Ogle, D. 1986. K-W-L: A teaching model that develops active reading of expository text. *The Reading Teacher* 37(6): 564-570.

Orlick, T. 1978. *The cooperative sports and games book: Challenge without competition.* New York: Pantheon Books.

Schrenko, L. 1994. *Structuring a learner-centered school.* Palatine, Ill.: IRI/Skylight Training and Publishing.

Shone, R. 1984. *Creative visualization.* New York: Thorson's.

Sternberg, R. J. 1985. *Beyond I.Q.: A triarchic theory of human intelligences.* New York: Cambridge University.

———. 1986. *Intelligence applied: Understanding and increasing your intellectual skills.* Boston: Harcourt Brace Jovanovich.

———. 1990. *Metaphors of mind: Conceptions of the nature of intelligence.* New York: Viking Penguin.

Williams, R. B. 1993. *More than 50 ways to build team consenus.* Palatine, Ill.: IRI/Skylight Training and Publishing.

Wood, A., and D. Wood. 1984. *The napping house.* New York: Harcourt Brace Jovanovich.

———. 1987. *Heckedy Peg.* New York: Harcourt Brace Jovanovich.

IRI/Skylight Training and Publishing, Inc.

Index

Learn from Our Books *and* from Our Authors!

Bring Our Author/Trainers to Your District

At IRI/Skylight, we have assembled a unique team of outstanding author/trainers with international reputations for quality work. Each has designed high-impact programs that translate powerful new research into successful learning strategies for every student. We design each program to fit your school's or district's special needs.

Training Programs

IRI/Skylight's training programs extend the renewal process by helping educators move from content-centered to mind-centered classrooms. In our highly interactive workshops, participants learn foundational, research-based information and teaching strategies in an instructional area that they can immediately transfer to the classroom setting. With IRI/Skylight's specially prepared materials, participants learn how to teach their students to learn for a lifetime.

Networks for Systemic Change

Through partnerships with Phi Delta Kappa and other organizations, IRI/Skylight offers two Networks for site-based systemic change: *The Network of Mindful Schools* and *The Multiple Intelligences School Network*. The Networks are designed to promote systemic school change as possible and practical when starting with a renewed vision that centers on *what* and *how* each student learns. To help accomplish this goal, Network consultants work with member schools to develop an annual tactical plan and then implement that plan at the classroom level.

Training of Trainers

The Training of Trainers programs train your best teachers, those who provide the highest quality instruction, to coach other teachers. This not only increases the number of teachers you can afford to train in each program, but also increases the amount of coaching and follow-up that each teacher can receive from a resident expert. Our Training of Trainers programs will help you make a systemic improvement in your staff development program.

To receive a free copy of the IRI/Skylight catalog, to find out more about the Networks for Systemic Change, or to receive more information about trainings offered through IRI/Skylight, contact CLIENT SERVICES at

SkyLight

TRAINING AND PUBLISHING, INC.
2626 S. Clearbrook Dr., Arlington Heights, IL 60005
800-348-4474 • 847-290-6600 • FAX 847-290-6609

There are
one-story intellects,
two-story intellects, and three-story
intellects with skylights. All fact collectors, who
have no aim beyond their facts, are one-story men. Two-story men
compare, reason, generalize, using the labors of the fact collectors as
well as their own. Three-story men idealize, imagine,
predict—their best illumination comes from
above, through the skylight.
—*Oliver Wendell*
Holmes

SkyLight
TRAINING AND PUBLISHING, INC.